HIDDEN HISTORIES

HISTORIES

—— HISTORICAL FIGURES ——

HIDDEN HISTORIES: HISTORICAL FIGURES

13-Digit ISBN: 978-1-64643-365-0
10-Digit ISBN: 1-64643-365-3

This book may be ordered by mail from the publisher. Please include $5.99 for postage and handling. Please support your local bookseller first!

Books published by Cider Mill Press Book Publishers are available at special discounts for bulk purchases in the United States by corporations, institutions, and other organizations. For more information, please contact the publisher.

Cider Mill Press Book Publishers
"Where good books are ready for press"
501 Nelson Place
Nashville, Tennessee 37214

cidermillpress.com

Typography: Abril Text, Ofelia Text

Printed in China

Vectors used under official license from Shutterstock.com.

23 24 25 26 27 TYC 5 4 3 2 1
First Edition

HIDDEN HISTORIES

—— HISTORICAL FIGURES ——

100 WILD STORIES
YOU NEVER LEARNED IN HISTORY CLASS

TIM RAYBORN

ILLUSTRATIONS BY REBECCA PRY

CIDER MILL PRESS

BOOK PUBLISHERS

CONTENTS

Introduction · **8**

COMPOSERS AND MUSICIANS

ARTISTS

ACTORS AND MOVIE STARS

OTHER ENTERTAINERS

ATHLETES

WORLD LEADERS

CRIMINALS AND SCOUNDRELS

SCIENTISTS AND INVENTORS

POLITICS AND MORE

INTRODUCTION

Human beings are a never-ending source of fascination, especially if they're famous. We all admire notable people from various walks of life (past and present), and sometimes we begin to feel like we know them, especially if we read all about them or follow them closely enough. But often those people have hidden parts of their lives that we never know anything about—which, honestly, is as it should be. After all, we have our own secrets and even dark sides, so why shouldn't they?

But sometimes, there are little-known stories about the lives of the famous and should-be famous that are fascinating, weird, wonderful, and too good to be true, and that's where *Hidden Histories* comes in. In this book, you will learn obscure facts about famous figures throughout history, as well as intriguing stories about people who deserve to be better known than they are. You'll discover the answers to questions like:

- What famous writer kept a pet bear at college?

- Members of which popular rock n' roll band once hung out with a notorious cult leader and murderer?

- Which noted artist would pull a gun on people who annoyed him?

- What actor found out as an adult that his "sister" was actually his mother?

- What teenager struck out one of the greatest hitters in major league baseball history?

- Which two women went from being slaves to becoming among the most powerful rulers in the history of the world?

- Which US president once saw a UFO?

- Which ancient philosopher hated beans?

- What teenage girl made a nighttime ride similar to Paul Revere's?

These and many more questions will be answered in the following pages. Explore the intriguing stories of the famous and the almost famous, and learn about the other sides of their lives that are often hidden, sometimes on purpose.

These tales are arranged in a number of convenient categories for your perusing pleasure. Feel free to dip into any entry you like and discover some hidden history!

CHRISTOPHER MARLOWE'S
ESPIONAGE MISSIONS

Most people who know the works of William Shakespeare probably have at least a passing familiarity with his fellow playwright, Christopher Marlowe (1564–93). Marlowe, a Cambridge-educated writer, was active in the late 1580s and early 1590s. His plays include such masterpieces as *Tamburlaine*, *Doctor Faustus*, and *Edward II*. While these aren't exactly household names like *Romeo and Juliet*, *A Midsummer Night's Dream*, or *Hamlet*, they are magnificent plays that hold up today and are still performed.

He was an undisputable genius, and had he lived longer, his work might even have outshone the plays and poems of Shakespeare. But he was destined to die a violent death at the age of thirty, in a tavern brawl over a dispute about the bill.

Or was there more to it than that? It is pretty obvious that, starting in his Cambridge days, Marlowe was more than just your typical university student. He seems to have been recruited by Queen Elizabeth's government to engage in spying missions. Danger abounded in the 1580s, and there were always plots against the queen's life. The queen's spymaster, Sir Francis Walsingham, was well aware of the dangers she faced, and sought out intelligent young men who could be put to work preserving the government and keeping the queen safe.

Indeed, in 1584–85, Marlowe had several long absences from his studies, longer than what would normally have been allowed. He also seemed to have a lot of money to spend on food and drink, far more than a typical poor student would have. So where was he during those absences, and where did his money come from? It seems likely that he was recruited to go on government spy missions, and was paid pretty well for his troubles.

He definitely went abroad a few times, and was even arrested in the Netherlands and sent back to England, but he suffered no punishment and was soon released.

He later got into trouble over rumors of being an atheist (a crime in Elizabethan England). In May 1593, while he was being investigated on this charge (and was ordered to stay nearby), he found himself at an inn, where the argument over the bill broke out. One of the other men stabbed Marlowe in or above the eye with a dagger, killing him.

A lot of people thought that the timing was suspicious. Was it an accident, or did he know espionage secrets that powerful people wanted kept quiet? Did he even die at all? Some think that he faked his death so that he could secretly travel back to Europe and continue spying. Some even think that he continued to write plays in secret and sent them to—you guessed it— William Shakespeare, who published them as if he had written the plays himself. This is very unlikely to be true, but Marlowe might have slipped away, leaving behind one of history's great literary mysteries.

WILLIAM SHAKESPEARE'S
MISSING HEAD?

William Shakespeare (1564–1616) is buried in Holy Trinity Church, the parish church in his home town of Stratford-upon-Avon. As millions of visitors to the tomb have seen, there is a bust of him there (looking a bit bored) and a famous quote written above the tomb:

> "Good friend, for Jesus' sake forbear,
> To dig the dust enclosed here.
> Blessed be the man that spares these stones,
> And cursed be he that moves my bones."

This is a pretty clear warning: he's lying there, so let him rest in peace, or prepare to suffer a curse. King Tut would be proud! Most people probably don't give these words too much extra thought, but someone at some point must have decided to ignore them, just like all those grave robbers in ancient Egypt who had no concern for mummies' curses. You see, it seems that Shakespeare's skull is missing; his bones *have* been moved after all.

A magazine called *The Argosy* reported back in 1879 that The Bard's skull had been stolen as early as 1794, but how they came by this information is unknown. Most people would assume this was just made-up nonsense, written to sell copies of the magazine. But in 2016, archaeologists were surprised to learn that it might just be true.

During a survey with ground-penetrating radar, the team found that The Bard's body was only buried about three feet underground, and that there was a disturbance on the side where the head should be. It looked like the ground had been dug up and then later refilled. They discovered bricks lying in that area, as if they were filling an empty space. The scan couldn't prove that there was no skull, but it seemed likely.

So if Shakespeare's skull really is missing, who took it and why? While we'll never know who, the "why" could very well be due to a silly pseudoscience called phrenology, a fad that was all the rage in the eighteenth and nineteenth centuries. This was the belief that you could measure someone's intelligence and talents by the shape of their head. Did some doctor want to have a look at Shakespeare's skull to find out what made him tick? It's possible. Or maybe someone just wanted a macabre souvenir from their Stratford vacation.

If his skull is truly missing, then it's lost forever, sadly, but maybe it eventually ended up as Yorick in a production of *Hamlet*. Shakespeare might have been amused by that, at least.

LORD BYRON'S
CAMBRIDGE BEAR

Lord Byron (1788–1824) was the original bad boy, a superstar of the literary world in early nineteenth-century England, and one who loved creating scandals. He had legions of fans, and women were said to swoon upon hearing his poetry, often even fainting if they saw him. It was like Beatlemania, but for a literary hero, and indeed, his wife, Annabella Milbanke, actually coined the word "Byromania." Another said that he was simply "mad, bad, and dangerous to know."

George Gordon Byron was the sixth Baron Byron, born into a world of wealth and privilege, though he had an unhappy childhood filled with neglect and even abuse. He had a somewhat malformed right foot, which made him self-conscious, though later in life he excelled at sports such as swimming, horseback riding, and even boxing.

And having a wealthy family meant that he received the best education that money could buy. In those days, of course, that meant going to one of the "big two": Oxford or Cambridge. Byron found himself at Trinity College in Cambridge between 1805 and 1807, and his rebellious streak was already on full display while there. He led a typical student's life of drinking and carrying-on, and had affairs with both young women and young men.

But something bothered him (there were probably several somethings, to be honest): the college had a prohibition against students keeping dogs as pets, which seems reasonable enough. But Byron was fond of his animal companions and felt that this was unfair. So, he decided to obtain and keep a pet bear instead! There was no university regulation against the keeping of a bear, so he flaunted the loophole and took his bear for walks (on a leash, of course) in town. That must have been quite a sight! Since he also came from a high-ranking aristocratic family, the university authorities weren't going to do anything to stop it and risk angering him or his family. So, a bear on a leash it was!

He obviously enjoyed rubbing the authorities' noses in it. In a letter dating from 1807, he wrote: "I have got a new friend, the finest in the world, a tame bear. When I brought him here, they asked me what to do with him, and my reply was, 'he should sit for a fellowship'."

When he left Cambridge, he took the bear with him to his estate. The college officials were probably just relieved to see him go! In any case, Byron kept a large number of dogs and cats. His favorite dog, Boatswain, contracted rabies, and Byron cared for him until he died. He also had a number of unusual animals, such as a fox, a monkey, a crocodile, some peacocks, and even some badgers. It was quite the menagerie, and worthy of the man who'd strutted around Cambridge with a bear.

MARY SHELLEY:
MORE THAN FRANKENSTEIN

Mary Shelley (1797–1851) is known around the world for her magnificent and monstrous creation in *Frankenstein*, and of course, it must once again be said: Frankenstein is the doctor, not the creature he made out of human body parts! The book came about when she and her husband, the poet Percy Bysshe Shelley, were visiting their eccentric friend Lord Byron in Switzerland. Kept inside by dismal summer rains, the assembled group decided to entertain each other by making up ghost stories. Mary's ideas would eventually take form in her novel, *Frankenstein; or, The Modern Prometheus*, which was published in 1818. Many now see it as the first true science fiction novel, and it is a classic that endures to this day. There are countless movie and TV adaptations of the story (some great, some not). Shelley's name will live forever in her warning about messing with the forces of nature, something we can appreciate perhaps even more today than at the time it was written.

But there was more to Shelley than just Frankenstein. She was the daughter of Mary Wollstonecraft, an important early feminist writer, who strongly encouraged proper education for girls, and believed that women were in every way equal to men. Unfortunately, she died just after young Mary was born, and when Mary Shelley's father remarried, she and her new step-mother didn't really get along. Young Mary had no formal education, but learned to read and would spend hours reading in the family's library, as well as by her mother's grave. As a child, she also liked to make up stories, a pastime that would stay with her for her whole life.

She wrote extensively throughout her life (novels, travel books, and more), though she faced the problem that most women authors did at the time; writing was not considered a "suitable" activity for women, so she had to have her books published anonymously, at least in the early years. In fact, since Percy wrote the introduction to *Frankenstein*, most people assumed that he'd written it! Percy died in 1822, leaving Mary a widow with a young child. The two had been living in Italy, but she returned to London, where she wrote for the rest of her life. Her work during this time included her novel, *The Last Man*, a story about a plague-devastated world (another subject that certainly resonates today).

She could never completely let Percy go. His body was cremated, but she kept his heart with her as a keep-sake. It had calcified and didn't burn, so she must have thought, "why not?" She carried it with her in a silk pouch, and after she died

PERCY
BYSSHE
SHELLEY
DIED 1822
"MARY...YOU HAVE MY HEART."

in 1851, the heart was found wrapped in one of Percy's poems in her writing desk drawer, which is about the most goth thing one can imagine!

EDGAR ALLAN POE'S
MYSTERIOUS DEATH

Edgar Allan Poe (1809–49) has delighted and chilled generations of readers with his tales of psychological and supernatural horror. He wrote immortal works such as "The Fall of the House of Usher," "The Tell-Tale Heart," "The Raven," "The Pit and the Pendulum," and many more. A pioneering early American writer, he told stories unlike anyone before him, and would influence writers of the horror and the supernatural ever after, including such luminaries as H.P. Lovecraft, Stephen King, and countless others. It's perhaps fitting that his last days were shrouded in mystery.

On the night of October 3, 1849, Joseph W. Walker, a Baltimore newspaper employee, found a man lying in a gutter outside of a local pub. This man was delirious, dressed in someone else's shabby clothing, and in a terrible state. It was Edgar Allan Poe. He managed to ask Walker to pass on a message to Joseph E. Snodgrass, an editor that had a medical background. Poe was attended to at Washington College Hospital, but he never fully regained his senses, and he died on October 7, allegedly from alcohol (Poe was an alcoholic) or brain swelling. On his last night, he kept calling out for someone named "Reynolds," a person no one has ever been able to identify.

A week before he was found in this terrible sate, Poe had left Richmond, Virginia to travel to Philadelphia to do some editing work. But no one saw him during that week, and he never made it to Philadelphia. What had happened? Where was he? How did he end up in such a terrible state that he died as a result? Unfortunately, we don't know, but there are some theories:

- He was beaten by an attacker and ultimately died of his injuries. He might simply have been mugged and left for dead.

- He was a victim of cooping, a fraudulent practice during elections (there was an election the day he was found). Gangs would seize people, dress them up, and force them to vote a certain way. The victim would then be "treated" with alcohol, dressed in different clothing, and sent to vote again under a different name. They would do this several times to the same person to pump up vote numbers. Poe, dressed in someone else's clothing and having a fondness for alcohol, might have fallen victim to a cooping scam.

- He died of rabies. Several of his symptoms were consistent with rabies infection, though no animal bites were noted on his body, but that information might have been lost over time.

- Poe had a brain tumor. Poe's erratic behavior could have been caused by something in his brain. More than two decades after he died, his body was exhumed to be moved to a more honored resting place, and one workman said that there was a clump of material inside the skull.

The brain would have been long gone, but a tumor might have calcified and still been in there.

- He was deliberately murdered. It's possible that the brothers of his new fiancée didn't like him and took him out.

- He had meningitis, which would explain some of his symptoms.

None of the explanations is completely satisfying, but his death might have been a combination of more than one. It's perhaps fitting that the man who wrote so many tales of mystery, suspense, and horror, would become entwined in a grisly mystery of his own at the end of his life.

JANE AUSTEN
WAS UNKNOWN DURING HER LIFE

Jane Austen (1775–1817) is one of the most famous writers in all of English literature. Her books, *Sense and Sensibility* (1811), *Pride and Prejudice* (1813), *Mansfield Park* (1814), *Emma* (1815), *Northanger Abbey* (1818, posthumous), and *Persuasion* (1818, posthumous), are beloved around the world by countless readers, and they've all been made into very pretty adaptations for film and TV many times. Her books are set in the Regency period of British history (1811–20) and offer a window into the lives of the upper-class of the time.

But as wonderful and well written as her books are, she faced the same problem that plagued so many other women writers of her day: writing was a job considered "unsuitable" for women, and publishers wouldn't put out books with women's names on them. So women had two choices: either adopt a male pen name, or have the book published anonymously. Austen opted for the anonymous choice, so her books appeared without any name at all. Of course, most of her readers just assumed that a man had written them.

Sadly, she was anonymous throughout her life, and didn't receive credit for her work until after she died.

There was one major exception to this, though. In November, 1815, the royal librarian, James Stanier Clarke, contacted Austen to inform her that no less than the Prince Regent himself was fond of her books and kept copies of them at his various homes. The prince ruled Britain at the time, because his father, King George III, was suffering from severe mental health problems; the prince was king in all but name. So how did he find out about Austen's identity? Well, when you're a king, you can do anything! Actually, Austen's brother had once been treated by a doctor who also treated the prince and told him who she was.

Clarke invited her to meet with him and told her that the prince "gave her permission" to dedicate her next book, *Emma*, to him. She didn't like the prince at all, but it was an offer she couldn't refuse. She tried to think up ways to get out of it, but eventually, she told the publisher to go ahead and put the dedication in the book, which was published in 1815. Sadly, she would die only two years later at the young age of forty-one, and her family arranged for her last two novels, *Persuasion* and *Northanger Abbey*, to be published after her death. Her brother added a note which finally identified her as the author of these and the previous books. In 1832, another publisher bought the rights to all of her works, and they've never been out of print since. But her fans today still wonder how many more amazing novels she might have written if she'd lived longer.

EMILY DICKINSON'S
RECLUSIVENESS

American poet Emily Dickinson (1830–86) lived in Amherst, Massachusetts. She was surprisingly unknown in her lifetime, but in the years and decades after she died in 1886, she has come to be seen as one of the most important American poets. She wrote more than 1,800 poems, but only a handful of them were published in her lifetime. The first volume of her poems wasn't published until 1890. And later in life, she was famously reclusive.

In her younger years, Dickinson was definitely social and had friends, but as she grew older, she increasingly withdrew from polite society, more intent on writing than in keeping up with socializing. And she wrote letters and poems prolifically throughout her life. By her thirties, having lived through much emotional turmoil (including caring for a chronically ill mother and losing various friends), she was content to stay inside at her father's home and avoid venturing out much, if at all. She never married, and if she did go out, she tended to dress only in white. Needless to say, it caused some gossip among the locals.

Her reclusiveness became almost legendary. She would spend hours at a time in her bedroom. If she had visitors, she would speak to them through the door, rather than opening up the door to see them, or (even worse!) coming down to the sitting room to greet them. When her father finally died, the funeral was held in the family home, and she didn't even come downstairs to attend, but rather, opened her bedroom door to be able to listen to it.

So why did she withdraw to such an extent, especially since she had been more social in her youth? Recently, some researchers have attempted to explain her reclusiveness as being caused by depression or anxiety, which are possibilities, though the true reason(s) will probably never be known. The important thing is that she continued to write letters to friends and colleagues, and she had her most productive years as a poet after she withdrew from the world. It's possible that she truly enjoyed the solitude and the chance to devote herself to her art without intrusions and distractions. In one of her poems from the early 1860s, she even mentioned that she "sneered" at the idea that her life was "small," and presumably at the towns-people who thought that of her. Whatever her reasons, she left the world a priceless poetic legacy that still captures readers more than 130 years after her death.

OSCAR WILDE'S
ECCENTRICITIES AND TRAGIC END

Oscar Wilde (1854–1900) was a gifted author, poet, playwright, and observant humorist who loved to shock, entertain, and call out the hypocrisy of the Victorian world that he inhabited with such gusto. He is known for his many humorous writings and plays, as well as his dark supernatural novel, *The Picture of Dorian Gray*. The main character, handsome young Dorian, makes a pact with a demonic force to remain forever young, while a hidden painting of him gets older and more hideous as the years go by. It is a gothic masterpiece that explores topics many readers at the time would have been uncomfortable with. One review said that the story was, "heavy with the mephitic odours of moral and spiritual putrefaction." Not a book-of-the-month club pick, then?

Wilde lived life on his own terms, and sometimes had run-ins with the law. His play *Salomé*, for example, retells the story of the infamous dancer who wanted the head of John the Baptist on a platter. But British law made it illegal to show any biblical characters on stage, so he was forced to move the production to Paris, where it was staged in 1896. It was written in French, so that was probably a better option anyway.

He was also homosexual in a time when it was illegal, and this led to his downfall. He made an enemy of the Marquess of Queensberry, whose son was having a secret affair with Wilde. The Marquess hired private detectives to spy on Wilde and was finally able to prove his claim. Wilde was tried and sentence to hard labor in prison for two years, from 1895 to 1897. This time took a terrible toll on him, and after he was released, he suffered from all sorts of health problems.

He left Britain and settled in Paris, but his days were numbered, as his health got worse and worse. Still, he kept his sense of humor. There are different stories about his last days in the hotel room where he died. In one he says, "Either these curtains go, or I do," while in another, he remarked, "This wallpaper will be the death of me—one of us will have to go." Both might be false, but they might be true.

He died in 1900 of cerebral meningitis, a victim of the hard labor he'd been forced into. In 1909, his remains were buried in the Père Lachaise Cemetery in Paris, and it wasn't long before fans and admirers were flocking to the grave. Over the years, his stone tomb became covered with lipstick kisses. In 2011, the city finally arranged for it to be cleaned, and walled it off behind glass. But the kisses kept on coming, and now the glass gets covered, though at least it's easier to clean! Wilde would probably be amused.

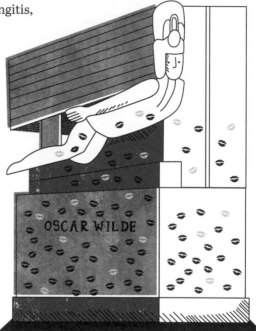

SIR ARTHUR CONAN DOYLE,
SÉANCES, AND FAIRIES

Sir Arthur Conan Doyle (1859–1930) had many professions and interests, including being a writer, a physician, a football (soccer) player, and a boxer. He wrote about a variety of topics throughout his life, including his sci-fi/fantasy book, *The Lost World* (wherein explorers discover a lost land filled with dinosaurs). But of course, he's best known for his wonderful creation,

Sherlock Holmes, whose adventures covered four novels and fifty-six short stories. Fun fact: he killed off Holmes in his 1893 story, "The Final Problem." Holmes and his nemesis Moriarty plunge to their deaths over the Reichenbach Falls in Switzerland. But fans weren't happy at all. There was a huge protest of angry letters and cancellations of subscriptions to *The Strand Magazine*, which published the stories. Doyle was eventually convinced to bring back Holmes in *The Hound of the Baskervilles* and in more short stories. The thing is, the popularity of these stories earned him enough money to pursue his other passion: Spiritualism.

Despite his training as a doctor—and the fact that Holmes relied on logic and rationality to solve crimes—Doyle was deeply interested in the Spiritualist movement. Spiritualism was a popular phenomenon at the time that involved mediums holding séances to try to contact the dead. It was all the rage in the late Victorian years, and Doyle was in the middle of it, firmly convinced that it was possible to contact the dead, if done properly. He was so devoted to the practice that it became a kind of religion for him and he left his Catholic beliefs behind to devote himself to Spiritualist ideas.

But his interests were broader than just spirits and ghosts. In 1917, two girls, Elsie Wright and Frances Griffiths, who lived in the village of Cottingley in West Yorkshire, made the amazing claim that they had actually photographed fairies in their garden, using their father's camera! Of course, many—if not most—people didn't believe them, but Doyle did. He became a champion for the girls' cause, claiming that they had done something extraordinary. He arranged for the photos to be analyzed at various labs, but the results were mostly inconclusive. Some researchers

thought that they might be authentic, while others insisted that they were not. Doyle remained a firm believer in fairies and the girls' story to the end of his life.

The question of whether the pictures were real wasn't settled until 1983, when one of the girls, now an old woman, admitted that they had faked the pictures, using cardboard cutouts held up with hatpins. Indeed, looking at them now, one can easily see that they are fakes. But, they said, the last photo they took actually was real. Frances said, "It was a wet Saturday afternoon and we were just mooching about with our cameras and Elsie had nothing prepared. I saw these fairies building up in the grasses and just aimed the camera and took a photograph." So maybe Doyle had been right all along? It sounds like a case for Sherlock Holmes!

D.H. LAWRENCE'S
NAKED TREE CLIMBING?

Lawrence (1885–1930) was a famed and controversial British writer, the author of books such as *Sons and Lovers*, *Women in Love*, and *Lady Chatterley's Lover*, all of which caused outrage and were the subject of censorship and trials. His works frankly explored sexuality in ways that were new and bold, and shocked "proper" society. He was hounded so much that he spent much of his later life in exile, leaving Britain behind in 1922 and traveling throughout Europe and then to Australia. He and his wife intended to settle in the United States, but his poor health made them decide to return to Europe, and he spent his last years in Italy, though he died in France. At the time of his death, many saw him as a talented writer who had wasted his abilities by writing smut. Happily, later evaluations have restored his status to reflect the literary genius that he was.

Lawrence had a deep love for nature, which shows in his writings. He seems to have had a special affinity for trees. He used to enjoy settling down and sitting against tree trunks to do his writing. While in Germany, he noted that the Black Forest was a stimulating location, and that he enjoyed the trees, which gave off "something dynamic and secret, and anti-human, or non-human." Being alone in nature is often appealing to those with an artistic bent, and he was no exception.

Beyond this, according to his obituary in the *New Yorker*, he liked to indulge in one particular activity that was definitely outside of the norm. The article claimed that Lawrence "had, among other eccentricities, a fancy for removing his clothes and climbing mulberry trees." Apparently, he was invigorated by doing this, and maybe it motivated his writing or improved his creativity. One can only imagine the shock that a group of walkers might have had, if they passed by a naked man sitting in a tree, awaiting inspiration!

Of course, many have said this story is nonsense, but it does seem to align with his frank views on sexuality and his affinity with the natural world and our place in it. The big question, of course, is why a mulberry tree and not, say, a maple, or an oak? A pine tree would definitely be uncomfortable, and a yew would be out of the question. If the story is true, he took the reason for choosing mulberry trees for his nude flights of fancy with him to his grave.

JOHN STEINBECK'S
DOGGONE PROBLEM

John Steinbeck (1902–68) was a Nobel Prize–winning author of such classics as *The Grapes of Wrath*, *East of Eden*, and *Of Mice and Men*. And it's that last novel in particular that resulted in more than a few problems during its creation. Steinbeck was immersed in his work in the mid-1930s. Of course, in those days, there were no computers or tablets or voice-activated anything. If you wanted to write, you sat down at a typewriter and pounded out your words, mistakes and all, or you picked up a pen or pencil and hand-wrote it out. Everything was stored in very vulnerable stacks of paper. There were no hard drives to back up your work on, so if you wanted an extra copy of your book, you or a friend had to write one. It was time-consuming and tedious.

Steinbeck had been making good progress on *Of Mice and Men*, but one spring day, a "minor tragedy" (as he put it) happened, involving his dog, Toby.

On May 27, 1936, he wrote to his editor:

> **"Minor tragedy stalked. I don't know whether I told you. My setter pup, left alone one night, made confetti of about half of my [manuscript] book. Two months work to do over again. It sets me back. There was no other draft. I was pretty mad but the poor little fellow may have been acting critically. I didn't want to ruin a good dog for a ms. I'm not sure is good at all... I should imagine the new little manuscript will be ready in about two months. I hope you won't be angry at it. I think it has some thing, but can't tell much yet. I'll get this off.**
>
> **I hear the postman.**
>
> **John Steinbeck"**

So the dog really did eat his homework! Or at least tore it to shreds as a new chew toy. Fortunately, Steinbeck seemed to take the whole thing in stride, but he had to start over again on a good portion of the manuscript. True to his word, Steinbeck finished a second draft two months later, and this time managed to keep the dog from eating it...

Of Mice and Men was published in 1937, and went on to be his first real success. Only two years later, it was made into a film, quite a ways to come from when a portion of the story was digesting in Toby's belly!

AGATHA CHRISTIE'S
MYSTERIOUS DISAPPEARANCE

British author Agatha Christie (1890–1976) was the master of murder mysteries, penning no less than sixty-six novels, as well as fourteen collections of short stories. She is acknowledged as one of the great masters of the art, and her characters such as Hercule Poirot and Miss Marple are practically household names. So it's probably only fitting that a great mystery surrounds the woman herself.

On the morning of December 4, 1926, Christie's car was found on a slope near Guildford in Surrey. The car's headlights were still on, and Christie's coat, as well as a suitcase, were still in the car, but the author herself was nowhere to be found. All signs pointed to an accident, perhaps even foul play. It was a mystery worthy of one of her own novels.

A missing person case always attracts interest, and soon this (at the time) little-known writer was suddenly on the front pages of newspapers. Many suspected foul play, and Christie's husband, Archie, was a prime suspect. Why? Well, he'd been having an affair with a woman named Nancy Neale, so there was obvious suspicion that he'd killed his wife. But if so, why would he be so sloppy about it? From the start, there were calls for a nationwide missing person search. Fellow author and noted believer in the paranormal, Sir Arthur Conan Doyle, even employed a psychic to try to locate Christie, giving said psychic one of Christie's gloves to help locate her (it didn't work).

Concern mounted, and the search picked up. Eleven days after her disappearance, a waiter at the Hydropathic Hotel in Harrogate, Yorkshire, noticed that one of the guests bore a strong resemblance to Christie and informed the police. The woman claimed to be from South Africa and went by the name Theresa Neale (does that last name sound familiar?). Archie and some policemen went to the hotel and waited for "Theresa" to make an appearance. She did, and sat down to read a paper with news about Agatha's disappearance still on the front page. Archie confronted her, and discovered that it was indeed his missing wife, but she seemed not to recognize him, though they'd been married for twelve years.

Two doctors would later state that she was suffering from amnesia, and perhaps a concussion, but the real reason for her disappearance is still debated. Was news of her husband's affair the cause? They had quarrelled the night before and she had left. Did she run off the road and suffer a concussion? If so, how did she make it to Harrogate (184 miles north) with enough money to stay for a week and a half? How was she not noticed before then? Did she have a nervous breakdown? Again, how did she end up so far away? Why did she genuinely not seem to recognize Archie at first? One biographer has suggested that she was in a "fugue" state, a kind of trance brought on by depression or trauma, and might even have been suicidal for a bit.

Or was it all a carefully-planned publicity stunt, a real-life mystery to bring attention to herself and her books, since she was planning on divorcing Archie for his affair, and needed to support herself? She and Archie did divorce and they both remarried; Christie's fame skyrocketed in better circumstances. She later wrote an autobiography (published in 1977, a year after her death), and she didn't mention the incident. So whatever happened, she took the truth with her, or maybe she didn't even know herself. Even Poirot couldn't solve this mystery!

THE 500 HATS (AND MORE) OF
DR. SEUSS

Theodor Seuss Geisel (1904–91) is known the world over for his wonderful, whimsical books and their instantly-recognizable drawings. As Dr. Seuss, he gave the world timeless classics such as *The Cat in the Hat* and *How the Grinch Stole Christmas*, among dozens of others, more than sixty in all. His books are delightful and silly, but also often deeply wise and filled with thought-provoking situations for children and adults alike.

One of his earlier books from 1938, *The 500 Hats of Bartholomew Cubbins*, tells the unlikely story of a peasant boy in medieval times who tries to remove his hat when the king walks by, but finds that there is still one on his head. This is mistaken for disrespect, but each time Bartholomew takes off his hat another one magically appears. Eventually, he goes through 500 of them, and toward the end, they get more elaborate and beautiful. It's a fun story with no great moral; the king simply keeps the hats in the end and rewards Bartholomew with gold.

But what most people probably don't know is that Dr. Seuss himself was a keen collector of hats throughout his life, including many that were completely ridiculous. He began collecting hats in the 1930s and kept up the hobby for the rest of his life. His obsession led to his writing *500 Hats*— his sister mentioned in 1937 that he had already collected a few hundred pieces of unusual headgear, and that they had inspired a new story idea.

He adopted several other unusual habits involving the hats over the years. He would wear various hats when he felt he needed new ideas and inspiration, and he would even insist his editors wear them when they were brainstorming, which must have made for some amusing meetings! But it was part of Seuss' charm, and his colleagues went along with it... most of the time.

Of course, one of his prized millinery possessions was his tall red-and-white striped top hat, the same kind as the one worn by the mischievous Cat in the Hat. Did the cat inspire the hat, or was it the other way around? Who knows? But the idea of him wearing a multitude of silly chapeau creations while working on his books and insisting that his friends do the same adds another delightful layer to a man who has brought joy to millions of readers of all ages.

COMPOSERS
AND
MUSICIANS

JEAN-BAPTISTE LULLY
ACCIDENTALLY KILLED HIMSELF

Lully (1632–87) was a very important composer at the court of the "Sun King," Louis XIV, in seventeenth-century France. His reputation was known far and wide, and he indulged the king by composing excellent ballets and operas, among many other works (the king had been a very good ballet dancer in his youth). Lully was also known to be pretty conceited, and he made more than few enemies during his life, though the king's favor always kept him out of too much trouble.

But he accidentally brought trouble upon himself while conducting one of his religious musical pieces, of all things. Back in those days, conductors didn't use the little baton like they do now. Instead, they held a staff and beat it on the floor to keep time. It so happened that in January 1687, while he was conducting some music he'd written to celebrate the king's recovery from an illness, he missed the floor and banged one of his toes pretty hard with the staff. It caused a wound, which he ignored, and which only got worse over the next two months. But his vanity kept him from having the toe amputated, as his doctor recommended. If he'd had that toe removed, he might have survived.

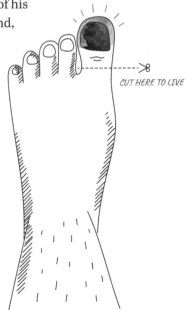

CUT HERE TO LIVE

But since disinfectants were unknown at the time, eventually a horrible infection, gangrene, set in and spread to the rest of his body. By March, he knew he was dying. A priest came to visit him and asked him to give up his sinful ways and repent. Lully responded by throwing the manuscript for his final opera on the fire and burning it up. Satisfied, the priest blessed him and left.

Seeing this, one of Lully's friends was shocked at the destruction of his last piece of music, and asked why he'd done it. Lully (making sure the priest was long gone) smiled and said that he had another copy! He died on March 22, a victim of his own carelessness and vanity.

FRANZ JOSEPH HAYDN'S
TWO SKULLS

The Austrian composer Franz Joseph Haydn (1732–1809) known as "Papa" Haydn to his friends and students, lived a long, happy, and prosperous life in the service of the wealthy Hungarian Esterházy family for most of his career.

When he was born, Handel and Bach were at the height of their creativity, and he outlived his younger friend Mozart by almost eighteen years. He even lived to see his student Beethoven begin to become a great composer in his own right. By any measure, Haydn's life was happy, but something very odd happened after his death.

He was given a funeral with great honors in Vienna on June 15, 1809, two weeks after he died. His body was buried in a churchyard close to where he'd lived, and that was the end of the matter, until 1820. In that year, Prince Esterházy requested that Haydn's remains be exhumed and buried at another church. This command was carried out on November 7, and should have been a routine job.

Only, something was wrong: Haydn's skull was missing. It seems that a few days after his death, a friend of his named Joseph Carl Rosenbaum, along with Johann Nepomuk Peter, a prison governor, conspired to do something terrible. They removed his head. Why would they do this? Because they were devotees of the silly pseudoscience called phrenology (which we discussed in Shakespeare's entry on page 12), and apparently, they wanted to examine

Haydn's skull for signs of genius. So when his body was found to have no skull all those years later, Rosenbaum sheepishly sent it back. However, he didn't send Haydn's actual skull, but someone else's!

Haydn's actual skull stayed in private possession for several decades and was finally donated to the Gesellschaft der Musikfreunde ("Society of the Friends of Music") in Vienna in 1895. The Friends of Music held onto it until 1954, when they finally saw to it that it was reunited with Haydn's body at last. The man who had lived such a happy life certainly had a strange afterlife!

In case you're wondering, we have no idea who the other skull belonged to, and yes, it also lies with Haydn's body, proving that two heads are, indeed, better than one!

CHOPIN'S
HEART AND BODY

Polish composer Frédéric Chopin (1810–49) was a remarkably gifted pianist and composer who delighted audiences with salon performance of his original works. He seemed to embody the spirit of the artists of the so-called Romantic Era: a moody genius who lived a dramatic and stormy life, and succumbed to tuberculosis at a young age, before his full promise as an artist could be realized.

He traveled throughout Europe, and his most famous companion was Aurore Dudevant, better known these days by her pen name, George Sand. Chopin was a musical celebrity, a concept that was new at the time but would endure in society ever after. His eventful and short life only added to his romantic reputation.

On the more macabre side, Chopin seemed to have an obsessive fear about being buried alive. Perhaps knowing that his health was not good, he wanted to ensure that nothing terrible happened before he was truly dead! Indeed, he left detailed instructions on what to do with his body after he died, just to be sure: he wanted his heart cut out and removed, so that he wouldn't accidentally wake up entombed somewhere and unable to escape. Basically, he didn't want to end up in a real-life Edgar Allan Poe tale!

After his death, his sister dutifully carried out his wish. She had his heart removed and placed in an urn, which was sent back to Warsaw. Once there, it was sealed up inside a pillar in the Holy Cross Church on the main street, the Krakowskie Przedmieście. Beneath the place where his heart rests is an inscription from the bible, Matthew 6:21: "For where your treasure is, there will your heart be also." His heart still lies there, even though the church was nearly destroyed in the bombings of World War II and had to be almost completely rebuilt.

As for the rest of his body? It's buried in Père Lachaise Cemetery in Paris, on a quiet avenue with trees and much greenery, a fitting resting place for a man who lived a tempestuous and all-too brief life.

HECTOR BERLIOZ'S
WILD MURDER-SUICIDE PLAN

The composer Hector Berlioz (1803–69) definitely led quite the interesting life. His most famous work is his *Symphonie fantastique*, which he admitted was inspired by an opium trip. The story tells of a young artist in love with a woman he cannot have, who then murders her and is sentenced to the guillotine for his crime. His own funeral then becomes a black mass and an orgy. Okay, then. His fellow composer Felix Mendelssohn said that the piece was "utterly loathsome," while Franz Liszt declared it a work of genius.

The thing is, the piece might be partly autobiographical, for Berlioz lived his own strange love story that almost led to his death. He had fallen for an actress, Harriet Smithson, but when she rejected him, he composed the *Symphonie fantastique* in response. But that wasn't the end of the story. In 1830, he met another woman, Camille Mokke, who agreed to marry him. He had to go to Italy to receive a prestigious prize he'd won and while there, Mokke's mother wrote to Berlioz, informing him that she was calling off their engagement and that her daughter was marrying another man, confusingly also named Camille.

Berlioz was enraged and began plotting to murder Mokke, her mother, and the other Camille as well. He devised an elaborate plan to dress up as a woman and enter their home in Paris, where he would shoot them all; then he would kill himself. Only, on the way back, he accidentally left his women's clothing on the train. He decided to kill himself by jumping off a cliff into the Mediterranean Sea near Genoa, but he landed in the water near a fishing boat and was rescued!

He started to change his mind, telling himself that Camille Mokke and her mother were not worth his time, anyway. He still pined for Smithson, and was actually able to arrange a meeting with her once he returned to Paris. Strangely, they hit it off this time, and she ultimately agreed to marry him in 1833.

But—no surprise—it was not a happy marriage. The real human being could never live up to his childish fantasy, and after eight years, he was having affairs. She took to drinking, and while Berlioz had moved on, he still supported her financially. She died in 1854, and he married his mistress, Marie Recio. But she died in 1862, and he soon fell in love with another woman, who died in 1864. He lived on for a few more years, but was broken and bitter, often wishing in his final years that death would simply take him away. In 1869, he got his wish.

ANTON BRUCKNER
AND BEETHOVEN'S CORPSE

Bruckner (1824–96) was an Austrian composer and organist known for his grand works. He was also a pretty strange fellow. His first real success didn't come until he was sixty years old. His seventh symphony really attracted attention, so he gets credit for persistence! He was a deeply religious Catholic, and would fall to his knees and pray whenever he heard church bells ringing nearby. He even did this in the middle of giving lectures.

He had a condition known as numeromania, which meant that he was obsessed with counting things, which some scholars say influenced his music and how long some of his works are (and they are long!). His greatest eccentricity, though, was his obsession with dead bodies; it might have even been an obsessive-compulsive disorder. He left detailed instructions for his own body to be embalmed after his death, and had a photograph taken of his dead mother, which he had framed and kept in his teaching room. Morbid as it might sound, these "death portraits" were not all that uncommon in the later nineteenth century. The body would be dressed in finery and photographed as if the person were alive and sitting for the photo. To be fair, it might be the only photograph of a family member that one would ever possess.

Bruckner's fascination with bodies spilled over into his obsession with his musical idol, Beethoven. When it was announced that Beethoven's remains were being disinterred from Vienna's Währing Cemetery to be reburied in the new Central Cemetery in 1888, and that the coffin would be opened, Bruckner knew what he must do: he *had* to see the body!

On the day, he arrived and pushed to the front of those gathered to get a good look. He went up to the coffin, picked up poor Beethoven's skull and cradled it and kissed it, before the horrified exhumers managed to retrieve said skull and pull him away, with a stern warning to stay back and get lost! On the way home, he noticed that one of the lenses from his eyeglasses had fallen out, presumably into the coffin. He was delighted to think that a piece of himself would be reburied with his hero. Some scholars now think that his obsession with the dead might have come from his deep belief in Catholicism, manifesting as an extreme version of relic veneration.

Oh, and once was not enough. Bruckner didn't just engage in this strange ritual with Beethoven's corpse; he also did it with composer Franz Schubert's body when it was reburied. In that instance, Bruckner would not give the skull back until he was allowed to place it back in the coffin himself. He was granted his wish, and *then* he was thrown out!

THE 27 CLUB

They say that only the good die young, which must really be true for rock and jazz musicians. There's a strange coincidence (curse?) out there involving popular musicians over the last several decades. There are now more than fifty "members" of the so-called "27 Club," musicians who died at the age of twenty-seven. Here are a few of the more famous examples:

- **Robert Leroy Johnson** (May 8, 1911 – August 16, 1938): An early blues guitarist that many later rock musicians name as hugely important for the blues genre. He died after drinking whiskey that might have been poisoned. He was allegedly flirting with a married woman, and her jealous husband spiked his drink with strychnine, though it might just be a rumor. Another legend about him says that he sold his soul to the devil at a crossroads for his musical abilities. He did like to practice in a cemetery at night, so who knows?

- **Brian Jones** (February 28, 1942 – July 3, 1969): A founder and early guitarist for the Rolling Stones. He was found drowned in the swimming pool of his home. Though drugs and alcohol were probably involved, rumors persist that he was murdered. Apparently several things were stolen from his house, too.

- **Jimi Hendrix** (November 27, 1942 – September 18, 1970): The legendary rock guitarist, whose influence is still heard in new generations of guitarists even today. He apparently overdosed on sleeping pills and choked on his own vomit, though many now believe that foul play was also involved.

- **Janis Joplin** (January 19, 1943 – October 4, 1970): A singer-songwriter and major act at the Woodstock Festival. Like many of her friends, she used heroin, and she died of an overdose.

- **Jim Morrison** (December 8, 1943 – July 3, 1971): The lead singer of the Doors. Officially, his cause of death was heart failure, but many suspect it was actually a heroin overdose. Several controversies remain surrounding his death. Some even claim that he didn't die, and faked the whole thing to disappear into a private life. His grave in Paris' Père Lachaise Cemetery is a pilgrimage site for his legions of fans.

- **Ronald "Pigpen" McKernan** (September 8, 1945 – March 8, 1973): A founding member of the Grateful Dead, he was afflicted with congenital biliary cirrhosis, which is an autoimmune disease of the liver. He died of a gastrointestinal hemorrhage.

- **Kurt Cobain** (February 20, 1967 – c. April 5, 1994): The lead singer of mega-star Seattle-based grunge band Nirvana, he killed himself with a shotgun to the head. However, there have been many conspiracy theories (some credible) insisting that he was murdered and his death was made to look like a suicide. Rumor has it that Cobain had actually been interested in "joining" the 27 Club.

- **Amy Winehouse** (September 14, 1983 – July 23, 2011): A very popular jazz and R&B vocalist, who won an amazing five Grammy awards in one ceremony. But she struggled with substance abuse and mental health issues, as well as legal troubles, and was found dead by her bodyguard. Her death was said to be due to alcohol poisoning.

THE BEATLES AND THE ROLLING STONES:
SLEEPY CREATIVITY

The Beatles and the Rolling Stones are without a doubt two of the most famous and influential rock bands ever. As part of the 1960s "British Invasion," their music and performances transformed the pop culture landscape and changed popular music forever. While the Beatles stopped giving public concerts in 1966, the Rolling Stones would keep on jamming live for the next half century and beyond. Whether you're a fan of either group, there's no doubt that both have enormous staying power and song-writing ability.

The funny thing is that members of both bands were inspired by dreams to write songs.

By 1967, there was a lot of tension among the members of the Beatles, and Paul McCartney, perhaps most of all, was feeling the pressure. The band's manager, Brian Epstein, died in 1967. He'd been such a driving force for the Beatles that now there was a feeling that they were adrift.

McCartney was hit hard by it, and it brought up memories of his mother, Mary, who had died in 1956. He later said: "One night during this tense time I had a dream I saw my mum, who'd been dead ten years or so. And it was so great to see her because that's a wonderful thing about dreams: you actually are reunited with that person for a second; there they are and you appear to both be physically together again. It was so wonderful for me and she was very reassuring... In the dream she said, 'It'll be all right.' I'm not sure if she used the words 'Let it be' but that was the gist of her advice, it was, 'Don't worry too much, it will turn out OK.'"

Yes, the dream inspired the song "Let it Be," and the "Mother Mary" of the song was his own mom, telling him that everything would be fine.

As for the Rolling Stones, guitarist Keith Richards had an unusual experience while sleeping one night. He explained: "I go to bed as usual with my guitar, and I wake up the next morning, and I see that the tape is run to the very end. And I think, 'Well, I didn't do anything.'" Thinking he'd accidentally hit the record button while sleeping, he played it back, "and there, in some sort of ghostly version, is [a version of '(I Can't Get No) Satisfaction']... after that, there's forty minutes of me snoring. But there's the song in its embryo, and I actually dreamt the damned thing."

So Richards literally dreamed up the Stones' most famous song, and recorded part of it in his sleep!

ELVIS PRESLEY'S
TOP-SECRET SECRETS

The King of Rock n' Roll had (and still has) legions of fans. In December, 1970, Elvis Presley (1935–77) was even able to arrange a meeting with then-President Nixon. Elvis collected police badges and wanted to add a Federal Bureau of Narcotics badge to his collection. He apparently thought this would also give him the freedom to transport drugs freely to any other country. During the meeting, Elvis told Nixon that he thought the Beatles had helped promote anti-American sentiment, and that instead, he was at Nixon's service, having studied communist brainwashing techniques. He asked the president if he could have a Bureau of Narcotics badge. "Can we get him a badge?" Nixon asked his aid, who said yes. Elvis was delighted, but kept the meeting secret. And that encounter wasn't the strangest thing about his life.

His death in August 1977 stunned the world. At first, it was said that he'd died of a heart attack, though that seemed weird to some people, including other doctors. A report issued a few months later said that he had up to fourteen different prescription drugs in his system, meaning that he either died of an overdose, or that the combination of that many drugs was lethal. Indeed, that year alone, his doctor had written more than 10,000 (!) prescriptions for various drugs, though incredibly, said doctor was later found not guilty of killing the King.

Still, many people weren't happy with the explanation, either. Some even began to think that he had faked his death to get away from the limelight and live out his life peacefully. While it smacks of crazy conspiracy theory, a few serious researchers have uncovered some interesting things about Elvis' life that are unusual, to say the least. One theory found evidence that Elvis might have feared for his life after receiving threats from the mafia, and that he had been secretly working with the FBI to help bring down an organized crime ring called "The Fraternity." Researcher Gail Brewer-Giorgio even wrote a book about this in 1988, titled *Is Elvis Alive?* that seemed to provide evidence for Elvis' anti-mob activities, though of course, not everyone agreed.

Still, there was talk of seeing a black heli-copter landing at Elvis' home, Graceland, in the dawn hours before his body was said to have been found. A former employee at Graceland even managed to get a photo of it. Did Elvis escape to some unknown location in this helicopter? Was he on the run? We don't know. There were even reports that his body looked strange, as if it was covered in wax. Was it the body of someone else, hidden under a fake wax Elvis mask? Again, no one can say for sure. Did Elvis die in August of 1977? Probably, but some unanswered questions about his secret life remain.

THE BEACH BOYS
AND CHARLES MANSON

Now this is not a pairing you would expect! But the truth is that before his infamous murders, Charles Manson (1934–2017) was deeply involved with several famous rock and pop bands in the mid- and late sixties, and was an aspiring songwriter himself. He attended their parties, jammed with them, and even wrote his own music.

Dennis Wilson (1944–83), drummer for the Beach Boys, was introduced to Manson in early 1968 via two of the young women in his cult. Manson and Wilson hit it off, and Wilson started hosting events at his lavish southern California home for Manson and his followers, parties filled with music,

LSD, sex, and more. It wasn't long before Manson and his groupies and cult members, known as "the family," were basically inviting themselves to stay at Wilson's home forever.

Manson was a wannabe rock star. He played guitar adequately and fancied himself a brilliant musician and songwriter. Wilson even introduced him to various other stars and industry bigwigs, but nothing much ever came of it and the family's behavior took a much darker turn. Fellow Beach Boy and brother Brian Wilson didn't like what he was seeing, but Manson warned him to back off. Dennis continued to live with the family camping out in his home, whether he wanted them there or not (and by now, he didn't). The family was spending his money, and it seemed like Manson had extended his cult powers over Wilson, who even signed him to the Beach Boys' record label, since no one else was interested.

After several months, it seemed like Wilson had had enough, and he was frightened enough to leave behind the whole house. He would later claim that the family had murdered people, crimes that have never been conclusively tied to Manson and the family, and ones that were separate from the infamous Tate-LaBianca murders that made Manson famous. The family squatted in Wilson's house until they were eventually evicted when the lease expired.

While Wilson was trapped by the family, Manson wrote a song called "Cease to Exist," which is pretty ominous, since we know what was about to happen (though it actually seemed to be about the tensions that Manson saw in the Beach Boys at the time). Wilson actually liked the music, and, still trying to help out Manson (for whatever reasons), he offered to buy the rights to the tune so that the Beach Boys could record it. Manson, still under the delusion that he was going to be a star, happily accepted payment in money and a motorcycle. Wilson took the tune, changed some of the lyrics, and amended the title to "Never Learn Not to Love." It was included on their album 20/20. Manson was not credited, and the rest of the band didn't know he'd written much of the music.

Manson was furious about the lyric changes, and made more threats to Wilson, including by leaving a bullet on his pillow. Manson tried to get support from Terry Melcher, a producer at Columbia Records, whom he'd met several times, but Melcher was not impressed and withdrew a provisional recording offer. Manson resolved that he was going to have revenge on Melcher, using his cult. Melcher and his wife had lived at 10050 Cielo Drive, but moved away, fearing Manson's retribution. And who moved into that address soon after? Roman Polanski and Sharon Tate. When the family went to the house, they assumed Melcher still lived there, and murdered everyone there. Manson had never explicitly ordered the killings, it seemed, but his influence over his cult members made him guilty by association. Tate was the victim of a tragic misunderstanding and being in the wrong place at the wrong time.

After the murders, of course, anyone who'd ever had anything to do with Manson and the family immediately distanced themselves from him as much as possible. Dennis Wilson's life was never the same, and many people think he felt guilty about introducing Manson to the music scene and for what happened. He fell into alcoholism, separated from his wife, and drowned off the shores of Marina del Rey in 1983.

THE AMAZING
DOLLY PARTON

Dolly Parton is a beloved singer and songwriter, known mostly for her country music, though she's ventured into other styles as well. She's written over 3,000 (!) songs, been nominated for fifty Grammys (and won eleven of them), and released more than forty top ten albums. There's no doubt she is a megastar with millions of beloved fans, but beyond the music, her personal life is just as fascinating. Here are just a few things you might not know about her:

- **Her parents paid the doctor who delivered her with a sack of oatmeal.** They were very poor, owning only a one-bedroom cabin in Tennessee's Great Smoky Mountains. The cabin, which Parton later bought and renovated, didn't have electricity or running water.

- **She wrote her hit songs, "Jolene" and "I Will Always Love You" on the same day.** To be fair, she did say in 2017 that she "thinks" she wrote these tunes on the same day, but isn't 100% sure: "I assume that I wrote them at the same time," she said, "it could have been a day or two, but on that same cassette, and I usually fill those up pretty quick, so I think I probably wrote those the same night." "Jolene" was immediately popular, while "I Will Always Love You," became a smash hit in 1992, when Whitney Houston sang a cover version of it for the film *The Bodyguard*.

- **She once entered a Dolly Parton look-alike contest... and lost.** As you'll see later on, Charlie Chaplin allegedly had the same problem. Parton thought it would be fun to enter a drag queen Dolly look-alike contest on Santa Monica Boulevard, just to see how she would do, but the judges apparently thought she didn't look enough like herself! She didn't even come close to winning.

- **She founded a free library for children in 1995.** The Imagination Library offers free books for children in the US, Canada, the UK, and Australia. It was intended in part as a tribute to her father, who was illiterate. Parton funds a portion of this wonderful charity herself, and it also accepts donations.

- **She holds two Guinness World Records.** One for "Most Decades With a Top 20 Hit on the US Hot Country Songs Chart" and another for "Most Hits on US Hot Country Songs Chart by a Female Artist."

- **Her theme park, Dollywood, is the largest employer in Sevier County, Tennessee.** It's visited by fans from all over the world, though she has admitted that she's never been on any of the rides there. "I have a tendency to get motion sickness," she explained, adding, "also, I'm a little bit chicken."

- **The world's first cloned animal in 1996, a sheep, was named "Dolly" after her.** And what more of a tribute could you want?

OZZY OSBOURNE'S
LESSER-KNOWN PAST

As the original front man for Black Sabbath and then a hugely successful artist in his own right, Ozzy has been a staple of the hard rock/heavy metal scene since the 1970s. His outrageous antics (including biting the head off a bat), drug and alcohol issues, and general flamboyant behavior are legendary. He even had his own Emmy-winning reality show, which he's said he hates and will never watch. But there are a lot of things about Ozzy that the general public probably doesn't know:

- Ozzy didn't do well in school because of his dyslexia. He left at the age of fifteen and worked odd jobs, including as a tool-maker and a horn tuner. Looking to make some more money, he decided to try his hand at burglary. In order to hide his identity, he says, "My mate told me to wear gloves. I didn't understand, so I took fingerless ones like milkmen use." He managed to steal some baby clothes (accidentally, because it was too dark to see) and some T-shirts. He tried to steal a TV, but it was heavy and he left it behind while fleeing. He was arrested and sentenced to six weeks in Winson Green Prison because he couldn't pay the fine. Actually, his father refused to pay it, to teach him a lesson.

- From criminal to crime-fighter, Ozzy once tried to subdue a burglar in his English home. He was naked at the time (Ozzy, not the burglar). The thief escaped with Ozzy's wife's wedding ring, but it was later recovered with the help of the British TV show "Crime Watch."

- When Ozzy joined Black Sabbath, they were called The Polka Tulk Blues Band, which doesn't exactly strike fear into the hearts of anyone (unless you have a polka phobia). Also, they had a saxophone player. They changed the name to Polka Tulk, and then to Earth. But they decided to go with Black Sabbath. Another band at the time, Coven, had a song called "Black Sabbath," but Ozzy and the boys insist that they got the name from a horror film that was showing at a local cinema. Weirdly, Coven's bassist was named George Osborne, but he went by the name "Oz Osborne."

- He has dyslexia, which he admits is a big problem, but also says has made him very creative: "We think in unusual ways," he says in his autobiography. "But it's a very bad stigma to have, not being able to read like normal people can. To this day I wish I'd had a proper education. I think books are great, I do. To be able to lose yourself in a book is f***ing phenomenal. Everyone should be able to do it. But I've been able to get through an entire book only a few times in my life. Every blue moon this thing in my head will release, and I'll try to read as many books as I can, because when it closes up it goes straight back to the way it was, and I end up just sitting there, staring at Chinese."

- Ozzy was once at a White House Press Club dinner, and then-President George W. Bush said "Mom loves your stuff." He was referring to Barbara Bush, former First Lady and wife of former President George Bush. Was this true? If not, it should have been!

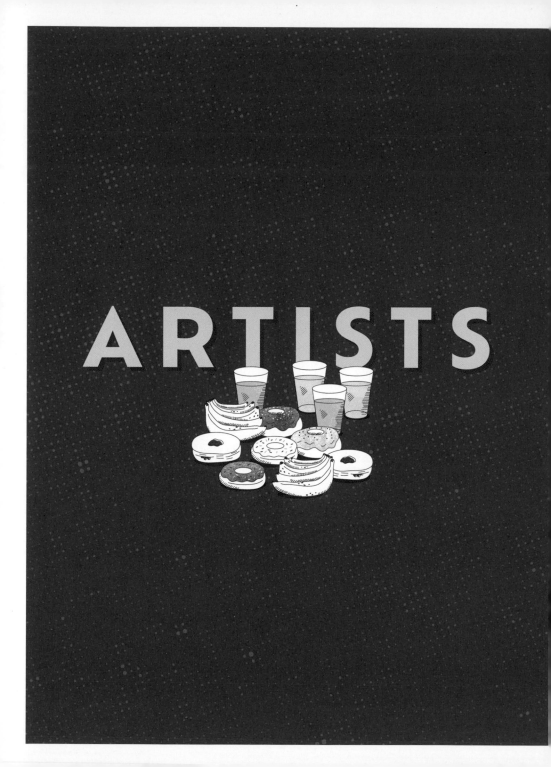

ARTISTS

MICHELANGELO'S
DIRTY LITTLE SECRET

Michelangelo di Lodovico Buonarroti Simoni (1475–1564), or "Mike" to his friends (okay, maybe not), is a world-famous, world-renowned artist, one of the greatest of the Italian Renaissance. Born in Florence, he lived an astonishing eighty-eight years and witnessed some of the greatest changes in European history; you know, the whole Renaissance thing, plus that little squabble about religion known as the Reformation.

Among his many masterpieces are the paintings in the Sistine Chapel in Rome (which, contrary to popular belief, he didn't paint lying on his back on scaffolding; he stood up on the scaffolds and leaned backwards as needed), numerous other paintings and sculptures, and even architectural designs. There is no doubt that he was one of the greatest artists to ever live, and his works have been an inspiration to generations of artists who have come after him.

But he had a dirty little secret. Well, it wasn't especially little, if anyone got too near him: he didn't bathe. Apparently, his father, Lodovico, had once told him never to wash himself. It was okay to rub himself down (get rid of dust and such), but he should never wash. Now you would think that most young people, especially if they were trying to win friends and influence people, would just shrug this piece of advice off with a "sure dad, whatever" response, but apparently Michelangelo took it to heart.

He didn't wash himself (and often not even his clothes), and was known to sleep in his work clothes and boots. Indeed, he pretty much never removed his boots at all. At some point, he developed gout and his feet and legs swelled. When a doctor came to examine him, he had to cut the boots off to get a better look. As he removed the boots, some of Michelangelo's skin came off with them. Gross.

Michelangelo was said to not only live in squalor, but also to have a rough and off-putting nature. Though he was totally devoted to art, his personality, combined with his terrible personal hygiene, meant that few, if any, young artists sought him out to study with him, certainly not for long periods of time. Even in an era when people didn't bathe all that often, his extra repulsive behavior kept people away. But it didn't seem to matter to him, and he had the last laugh, outliving most them!

SOFONISBA ANGUISSOLA: AN OUTSTANDING RENAISSANCE WOMAN

Sofonisba Anguissola (1532–1625) is one of the greatest artists you've probably never heard of. She was the first female artist to achieve a measure of international acclaim and recognition. Even artists like Michelangelo (he of the no-bathing lifestyle) respected her work. She was born in Cremona, Italy to an aristocratic family, which meant that she already had several advantages that those poorer than her wouldn't have had. Her father actually encouraged all of his children to take up artistic pursuits, and soon thereafter young Sofonisba showed a true talent for art.

Unfortunately, women were not allowed to become apprentices to artists— typical of the sexist garbage of the time. Fortunately for Sofonisba, her family was very rich and they could pay an artist to teach her privately. They employed an established painter, Bernardino Campi, to be her teacher, and he was more than happy to break with tradition and take their money! She grew as an artist under Campi and other teachers, and at the age of twenty-two, she went to Rome and met Michelangelo (she might have kept a scented handkerchief near her face, or something!). He recognized her ability when she showed him a picture of a laughing girl and he challenged her to draw a crying boy. She did, giving him a drawing of her brother that she titled *Asdrubale Bitten by a Crayfish*. The title alone makes you want to see it, doesn't it? Michelangelo was suitably impressed and even offered her a chance to look at his notebooks and copy out ideas in her own style.

Of course, art as a profession was still meant for men (she wasn't allowed to study anatomy, as it was considered inappropriate for women to do so), and it seems like her father had encouraged her talent to make her more "marriageable." Thanks, dad. In any case, her reputation was already growing, and in 1558, King Philip II of Spain sent her an invitation to come to his country and join his court. She was twenty-six at the time, and it must have been a dream come true. Her father, who had wanted her to advance in life through a good marriage, seemed pleased with this offer. In the fourteen years that Sofonisba stayed in Spain, she taught painting to the queen and the royal daughters. In 1571, she married a nobleman, Fabrizio Moncada Pignatelli, and they moved back to Italy in 1573. When Pignatelli died in 1579, King Philip gave her a royal pension for life, allowing her to live as she pleased and continue with her art. She later married a sea caption for love (hey, at that point, she could do whatever she wanted!) and lived to the ripe old age of ninety-three!

In 1624, a year before she died, the great Flemish painter Anthony van Dyck visited her and painted a last portrait of her. He said that in talking with her, he learned more about painting than from any other source. Her success and reputation opened doors for other women artists, who had for too long been denied a chance to thrive.

LEONARDO DA VINCI'S
ANIMAL INSTINCTS

Leonardo da Vinci (1452–1519) is remembered as one of the greatest artists of not only the Renaissance, but all of history. His world-famous Mona Lisa (more about her in the Picasso entry on page 64, believe it or not!) and his stunning drawings and other artwork have delighted millions of art lovers for centuries. The man himself was enigmatic and mysterious, and while we know a good deal about him, some feel that we can never truly *know* him. He was a brilliant artist and designer, but a notorious procrastinator, who left a surprisingly small number of paintings (only about thirty) that can definitely be attributed to him. But his designs for everything from tanks to flying machines show him to be a true "Renaissance man."

He was certainly an outlier in several of his beliefs. He was probably a vegetarian, an unusual practice for his time. We say "probably" because the evidence is not absolutely conclusive, though it seems to point that way. There have been some false quotes attributed to him (that's just the curse of the internet these days), but it seems that he might well have had objections to eating meat in principle, even as he was happy to design war machines (like the aforementioned tank) for the wealthy and powerful.

Others knew about this during his lifetime. An Italian explorer named Andrea Corsali once wrote about the Indian peoples and their religion of Hinduism: "Certain infidels called Guzzarati are so gentle that they do not feed on anything which has blood, nor will they allow anyone to hurt any living thing, like our Leonardo da Vinci."

Now, Corsali didn't seem to know Leonardo, which means that if this statement was true, the artist must have had something of a reputation as an oddball for not eating meat, and having an ethical problem with killing animals. Leonardo never unequivocally said that he did not eat meat, though he did slip things into some writings that might indicate it. In one instance, he was engaged in a contest where one needed to describe an everyday topic in a horrific way, and he had this to say about farm animals, such as cows and sheep: "Endless multitudes of these will have their little children taken from them ripped open and flayed and most barbarously quartered."

Was he really expressing discuss at animal slaughter? Or was he playing the game perfectly?

We don't know, but the fact that he chose this example might well be an indication of his thoughts on the matter. He does seem to advocate for animal welfare in his notes, and the artist Giorgio Vasari wrote of him in his book, *Life of Leonardo Da Vinci*, published in 1550: "He delighted much in horses and also in all other animals, and often when passing by the places where they sold birds he would take them out of their cages, and paying the price that was asked for them, would let them fly away into the air, restoring to them their lost liberty."

Whatever the truth, it seems that Leonardo had a high regard for animals, far more than most of the people of his time.

CARAVAGGIO'S
VIOLENCE

Michelangelo Merisi da Caravaggio (1571–1610) was a famed Renaissance painter who spent a good portion of his life in Rome (after training in Milan), though in his last few years, he was forced to spend time in Malta and Sicily. Art historians praise his work for its realism and emotional power, as well as his amazing use of lighting. He could create striking images lit against very dark backgrounds (a technique known as tenebrism), and his paintings could sometimes be disturbing, depicting scenes of violence and death in new and shocking ways. He had a direct influence on the emerging style of Baroque and later art, and art historian André Berne-Joffroy even claimed: "What begins in the work of Caravaggio is, quite simply, modern painting." That's a bold statement!

All of this is fascinating, but what makes Caravaggio a perfect candidate for inclusion here is that his personal life was often as violent and turbulent as his paintings. He seemed to be very short-tempered and touchy, and could fly off the handle at the simplest things. He was known for getting into fights, and was detained many times. In the early 1590s, he allegedly killed someone (presumably in a fight) and had to flee Milan to escape a murder charge. He took up residence in Rome, but his troubles with the law were far from over.

He beat a nobleman with a club in 1600, and was arrested more than once for violent outbursts. He was not limited to physical violence, but once found himself in a lawsuit for defamation. He was also arrested for insulting city guards and sued for throwing a plate of artichokes in the face of a tavern employee (another version says he hit the man in the mouth with the plate). He attacked a fellow artist (who had insulted him) with a sword, and was arrested for illegally possessing weapons. No one but noblemen were permitted to carry swords, but he did anyway, and had his blade inscribed with the phrase "Without hope, without fear."

It all just kept getting worse. In 1605, he had to flee to Genoa for a while because he injured a notary over a dispute about Lena, his model and lover at the time. His patrons were able to intervene and smooth things over, allowing him to return. When he came back to Rome, his landlady sued him for unpaid rent. He responded by throwing rocks at her window. She sued him again. Another time, he threw rotten vegetables at her and more than once threatened to kill any artists who copied his style.

In 1606, his behavior finally caught up with him. He killed a man and again fled to escape a murder charge. The circumstances of this situation were gruesome. He fought a duel with a gangster, Ranuccio Tommasoni, and mutilated him by castration before killing him. He had to leave Rome to avoid execution, and managed to join the Knights of Malta in 1607, hoping for a papal pardon. In 1608, he was expelled from the order for being a "putrid and fetid member." He went to Sicily and then back to Naples. But he was attacked there, and his face was badly disfigured. In 1610, he made for Rome, still hoping for his pardon, but he died, possibly of malaria, or possibly of lead poisoning (which might explain his erratic and violent behavior). Or perhaps the Tommasoni family hunted him down.

His legacy to the art world is undeniable, but his violence is so outrageous that one truly wonders what kind of tortured soul dwelled behind the artistic genius.

VAN GOGH'S
MISSING EAR MYSTERY

Just about everyone knows the story of how artist Vincent Van Gogh (1853–90) cut off his ear. He did it on December 23, 1886, after a feud with fellow artist, Gauguin, when they were working together. He threatened Gauguin with a knife and then turned it on himself. Afterward, he was said to have wrapped the ear in a cloth and offered it to a local prostitute. It's all bizarre and pretty gross, but art historians and enthusiasts have long wondered if he actually did it. Well, the answer is a bit less clear than you might think.

That Van Gogh did something to himself is certain. He was in a state of severe depression and disturbance, and was (obviously) not acting rationally. But just how much of his ear did he manage to remove? There are conflicting stories about that. Jo Bonger (his sister-in-law) wrote that he had only cut off part of his ear. He stayed with her in Paris in 1890, so she would have seen the effects of the damage. But she also wrote about it many years later (in 1914) and might have wanted to preserve his memory by downplaying the injury.

Three months after the incident, the artist Paul Signac met with Van Gogh and described the wound as being limited to his ear lobe. Conversely, Paul Gachet Jr., the son of Dr. Paul Gachet (Van Gogh's best friend in Auvers-sur-Oise) wrote that the wound, "was not all the ear [but] it was a good part of the outside of the ear (more than the lobe)."

These somewhat conflicting reports do seem to indicate that it was only a lower portion of the ear, possibly a little more than the lobe. But other versions say differently. Gauguin himself seems to have seen the damage the day after the incident, and later told a fellow artist in Paris that it was much of the whole ear. He said the same thing again in his memoir of 1901. A policeman named Alphonse Robert also reported that Van Gogh had cut off his whole ear. Dr. Félix Rey, who treated Van Gogh, would later (in 1930) draw a sketch of the wound, showing that it was pretty much the entire ear.

But there is some evidence that Rey's memory was not so good by the time he made that sketch. His description of Van Gogh himself, for example, was not at all accurate. Other witnesses later would claim it was the upper portion of the ear, not the lower.

You would think that an episode as dramatic as this would be pretty straightforward, but clearly, there are several different versions of this story. If Van Gogh removed the whole ear, he might have been trying to kill himself by bleeding to death. If it was only a portion, he might have been expressing his frustration while in a disturbed state. Van Gogh certainly did something terrible to himself in a fit of rage and depression, but the extent of that injury might never be known.

RENOIR'S
CRIPPLING PAIN

Obviously, artists need their hands to work. Whether they are painters, sculptors, or they work in some other visual medium, use of their fingers, hands, and arms is essential. So when an artist is struck down by a limiting physical condition, it can be tragic, devastating, and unbearable. Such was the case with Pierre-Auguste Renoir (1841–1919), one of the leading French impressionists of the late nineteenth and early twentieth centuries. For the last few decades of his life, he was stricken with severe rheumatoid arthritis, which, given the limitations of treatments at the time, meant that he was in almost constant pain.

People who met him and knew nothing about him other than what they'd seen in his art were often shocked. He continued to paint even while suffering terrible pain and navigating the deformity that his condition caused. Witnesses described his gnarled and stiffened hands as having the fingers bent down towards his wrists, and his thumbs bent inward, almost to the point of immobilization. People couldn't fathom how a man in this condition could still paint, and do it so well. Some wondered how he could even hold a brush.

At times, he could barely move at all. A film from 1915 shows Renoir at age seventy-five seated in a wheelchair (by then, he couldn't walk), holding a brush at a canvas, while his son stands by to arrange the palette and place other brushes in his father's hand, a hand that is clenched shut. Somehow, Renoir was able to continue to paint, even though he could barely hold his tool. Renoir also needed help with the canvasses themselves, since his arms could only move so far.

The film was made by Sacha Guitry in 1915 as a counter to German propaganda about Germany having all the best arts and culture. Guitry wanted to highlight the masters of French culture, and a disabled Renoir fighting against the odds was a perfect choice. At one point, he asked Renoir about the pain and expressed his sympathies. Renoir responded that yes indeed, his foot was in pain! He then proceeded to paint, even though his hands were clenched and withered; he was still determined to bring his artistic works to the world.

Renoir died in 1919, wracked with arthritic pain, but dedicated to creating art to the last. The artist Henri Matisse once asked him why he bothered to continue painting in his condition, to which Renoir replied, "The pain passes, but the beauty remains."

CLAUDE MONET
HAD THE BLUES

Claude Monet (1840–1926) was a long-lived French painter who was a founder of the Impressionist school and a forerunner of modernism. His colorful and vibrant paintings are admired by art lovers the world over, and can be seen in many galleries of the greats. Impressionism focused on changing light and perception, rather than super-realistic paintings. The term actually came from one of Monet's own works, *Impression, soleil levant* ("Impression, Sunrise"). An art critic named Louis Leroy coined the term "Impressionism" as part of satirical review he wrote for the newspaper, *Le Charivari*. Leroy intended it to be an insult, but it soon caught on and was adopted not only by artists, but composers and writers as well. So who had the last laugh?

Monet was a champion of the style and continued to work throughout his life, but in his later years, he was afflicted with a problem that any artist of the time would have dreaded: cataracts. He was diagnosed with them in 1912, and was advised that he should have surgery to remove them, but he refused, fearing that his eyes might be damaged and he might lose his ability to see color.

But by not having them removed, his vision became blurrier and he lost the ability to see some colors anyway. These impairments showed up in his works, as his brush strokes got broader, his colors got darker, and blue disappeared almost entirely from his palette. He had to take to labelling his paints because he couldn't tell what colors some of them were. In 1918, he wrote: "I no longer perceived colors with the same intensity. I no longer painted light with the same accuracy. Reds appeared muddy to me, pinks insipid, and the intermediate and lower tones escaped me."

He finally agreed to have the surgery in 1923, which improved things greatly, though for a time he suffered a common side effect, cyanopsia, where everything was tinted blue. So he went from having trouble seeing blue at all to seeing it everywhere! "I see blue," he wrote more than a year after the surgery. "I no longer see red or yellow. This annoys me terribly, because I know these colors exist." He took to wearing tinted glasses to help him see those missing colors again.

But overall, the surgery was a success, and he went back and reworked some of the paintings he'd made over the previous decade, to add in blues and make them a bit more like he'd intended them to be. Still, he hated some of them and ended up destroying them, to the dismay of art lovers everywhere!

PICASSO
THE GUN-TOTING ART THIEF

Picasso (1881–1973) was baptized Pablo Diego José Francisco de Paula Juan Nepomuceno María de los Remedios Cipriano de la Santísima Trinidad Martyr Patricio Clito Ruíz y Picasso, but he wisely chose to use his first and last names only. Imagine having to write out "Pablo Diego José Francisco de Paula Juan Nepomuceno María de los Remedios Cipriano de la Santísima Trinidad Martyr Patricio Clito Ruíz y Picasso" every time you wrote a check. And yes, there will be a test on this at the end of the book.

Picasso is best known for his striking artistic style, Cubism, with its angular lines and facial features in the wrong places. Art historians regard him as one of the most important artists of the twentieth century, but did you know that he also added "gun-wielding art thief" to his list of accomplishments?

Well, that might be a bit of an exaggeration, but Picasso had little patience with people, and he got tired of being asked the same questions over and over again. So, he took to carrying a Browning revolver (it had once belonged to the surreal French playwright, Alfred Jarry, who used to bring pistols to parties). Picasso loaded it with blanks and kept it with him at all times, so that he could "shoot" anyone who he decided was annoying or dull. Anyone who didn't know that he did this was probably in for a nasty shock when he hauled it out and pointed it at them!

As if this wasn't odd enough, he once found himself in the middle of an art theft scandal. A big one. On August 21, 1911, the *Mona Lisa*, Leonardo da Vinci's masterpiece, was stolen from the Louvre Museum in Paris. Soon after, an artist, Joseph Géry Pieret, came forward to accuse Picasso and his friend, the poet Guillaume Apollinaire, of having sculptures that had been stolen from the Louvre. Pieret had actually stolen these pieces and sold them to Picasso, who claimed he knew nothing of their origin, even though they were marked as property of the Louvre!

Of course, this also made Picasso and Apollinaire prime suspects in the *Mona Lisa* theft, but after Picasso returned the statues and the two men were questioned in a court, they were released due to lack of evidence of any involvement. But a cloud of suspicion still hung over their heads.

Finally, in December of 1913, and no doubt to Picasso's relief, the *Mona Lisa* was found. An employee at the Louvre named Vincenzo Peruggia had stolen the famous smiling lady and had kept it in a trunk in his Paris apartment before returning it to Florence, Italy. He apparently thought that since Leonardo was Italian, the painting naturally belonged in Italy. The *Mona*

Lisa was recovered and Picasso was completely exonerated. News of the theft only made the painting more famous, elevating it to the status it now enjoys in the art world. It was exhibited around Italy before being returned to the Louvre.

NORMAN ROCKWELL
WEIGHS HIS OPTIONS

Norman Rockwell (1894–1978) is beloved for his painting of Americana, capturing the essence of a "more innocent time" in small-town America. Some critics found his work too sappy and not "serious" enough, but he delighted generations of fans, capturing moods with wonderful, realistic facial expressions in a way that few other artists before him had. And yet, he suffered from depression and his doctor once said that he "painted his happiness, but did not live it," a rather sad commentary. His works adorned the covers of *The Saturday Evening Posts* for decades (between 1916 and 1963), and he would paint an incredible 323 of those covers for the magazine throughout his career.

But one story from when he was a young man stands out for its oddity. When the US entered World War I in 1917, Rockwell was eager to sign up for the navy. But he had a problem: he was something of a beanpole and had too little weight for his height. So he was rejected for service. Now, he could have gotten depressed and given up, but he was determined to get in. Depending on who you believe, there are two versions of his solution. One says that he was eight pounds underweight and another that he was seventeen pounds underweight for his height.

According to the eight-pound version, he gorged himself on bananas, donuts, and liquids the night before another weigh-in and managed to pack on enough external fake weight to convince the navy medical officer to admit him. The other version also says that he used the trusted banana and donut method, but it doesn't say that he did it all in one night. Let's face it, that would probably have been impossible anyway, or at the very least, painful and possibly fatal. In both versions, he bulked up enough to meet the requirement.

The funny thing is, after he was admitted, he was put to work as an artist and never saw combat anyway, so his weight to height ratio didn't even matter!

SALVADOR DALÍ'S
BIG BOWL OF SURREAL

Dalí (1904–89) is one of the twentieth century's most famous artists in the surreal style. His weird, whimsical, and wonderful paintings, such as *The Persistence of Memory* (1931) have fascinated and intrigued viewers for decades. His landscapes are often quite detailed, but filled with impossible figures and designs. His work is very much like looking into the weird world of dreams, a realm where anything can be possible.

As you might expect, Dalí wasn't exactly boring in real life. His quirks and eccentricities could irritate people to no end, and he seemed to live up to his bizarre art by living a life that flouted rules and conventions, and delighted in doing it.

He firmly believed that he was the reincarnation of his dead brother. Before he was born, his parents had another son, whom they had named Salvador, but he died after suffering from stomach issues. When their next son was born, they thought he resembled their dead son so much that they named the new baby boy Salvador as well. As a young child, his parents told him about his brother, and Dalí later wrote that the older Salvador "was probably the first version of myself but conceived too much in the absolute." Later, he would work images of his dead brother into his artwork, including the obviously-titled *Portrait of My Dead Brother* in 1963.

As an adult, he exhibited a lot of strange behaviors, sometimes including violent outbursts. Once, while working on a display window for a department store in New York, he saw that someone had made changes to it that he hadn't approved. He became so angry that he shoved a bathtub through the plate glass window. When attending a film premiere at a New York gallery, he thought that the film almost exactly resembled an idea of his own, and pushed over the film projector. He admitted, "I never wrote it down or told anyone, but it is as if he had stolen it!" Apparently, the filmmaker had psychically poached the idea from Dalí's head.

Not everything he did was in anger, thankfully. He once showed up to the Sorbonne to give a lecture, only he did so in a Rolls-Royce that was filled with cauliflowers. When fans asked for autographs, he would give them, but then steal their pens. He would sometimes avoid paying in restaurants by drawing pictures on the checks, figuring that the restaurant owners would rather have his original art than his money. Honestly, he probably wasn't wrong!

For a time, he kept a pet ocelot, Babou, which he would take for walks, and would often appear in public with wielding a walking stick and wearing a long cape. He once said that every morning, he had the pleasure of remembering that he was Salvador Dalí, a privilege that no one else enjoyed.

He was admitted to the French Academy of Fine Arts in 1979 in recognition of his contributions to twentieth-century art. One of the other members said that he hoped this honor would put an end to Dalí's "clowneries." Pretty sure that didn't happen...

ANDY WARHOL'S
TIME CAPSULES

Andy Warhol (1928–87) was one of the most important and influential pop artists of the twentieth century. Though he's known for the quote, "In the future, everyone will be world-famous for fifteen minutes," he might or might not have actually said it; it's possible that a photographer named Nat Finkelstein came up with a version of the phrase instead while photographing Warhol in 1966. In any case, Warhol changed the way that the world thought about what art was and could be. And he offered a fascinating way to learn about him and his processes.

Over the course of the last thirteen years or so of his life, he made over 600 "time capsules," which were basically whatever he felt like putting into a cardboard box at that moment and sealing up. They were meant to be snapshots of his life at a given time, and they have revealed an astonishing variety of different things—weird, whimsical, and everything in between. The entire project was meant to a be a work of art, and curators and historians at the Andy Warhol Museum in Pittsburgh have spent years delving into its details.

A lot of the contents are, to be honest, just everyday items: fliers for art galleries, letters, items that people sent to him, postage stamps from old envelopes, candies, and even a piece of concrete. And of course, there have also been Campbell's soup cans! The boxes have also included not-so-great things like nail clippings, a mummified foot, dead insects, and even used condoms!

But there have also been some treasures in them, like genuine works of art that had not seen the light of day before and are now valued at huge amounts of money. There seemed to be a method to his madness; it wasn't just a case of throwing in whatever he felt like in the moment. As such, each unboxing has been an event that has excited the art world about what might be found next.

The Andy Warhol Museum has also sponsored recent projects such as the Gen-Z Time Capsule, featuring artwork, pictures, and more from 1997–2012 in its exhibit. Topics include politics, photography, art and music, the internet and social media, fashion, technology, sports, mental health, and animals. It's all designed to give a unique window into those fifteen years. Warhol's idea of capturing the everyday for posterity lives on!

THE MYSTERY OF
BANKSY

"Banksy" is the pseudonym of an unknown street artist based in England (though his work has shown up all over the world) who has been delighting and mystifying people since the 1990s. His graffiti features paintings in stencil form, and can be imbued with political, satirical, and subversive messaging. He paints on walls and sidewalks, and occasionally other structures, including his own purpose-built objects, but always for public viewing.

Of course, his secret identity makes him all the more interesting. Obviously, one of the main reasons he has done this is because graffiti is, technically, illegal, but it's also allowed his legend to grow. There have been many speculations about who he might be. One is a man named Robin Gunningham, from the town of Yate north of the city of Bristol, and several of his old classmates have confirmed that he is indeed the artist. But not everyone is so sure.

There have been many other possible candidates, including Robert Del Naja (3D), a member of the band Massive Attack, who at the very least is a friend of Banksy's. Another is Billy Gannon, a member of the council of Pembroke Dock, a town in southwest Wales. He ended up resigning over the whole controversy because he said it interfered with his duties. "I'm being asked to prove who I am not, and the person that I am not may not exist," he said in explanation. Another interesting candidate is Paul Gough, vice president of Arts University Bournemouth. He is writing a book about Banksy, and who better to write this book than the man himself? He has taken it all with good humor, even though some of his students are now convinced he is the missing man. An artist himself, Gough even admitted that a collaboration between him and Bansky would be an "interesting prospect." Asked if he is actually Banksy himself, Gough simply replied, "no comment." He was probably just having fun. Maybe...

The mystery of Banksy's identity is part of what makes him so interesting, and why he remains in the public eye, even after decades of producing street art. Everyone likes a good mystery, and sometimes, it's better if these remain unsolved. He has even been nominated for awards recognizing his social significance, though it's highly unlikely that he would ever show up to collect them if he did win!

ACTORS AND MOVIE STARS

CHARLIE CHAPLIN'S
FAILED LOOKALIKE
CONTEST ENTRY

Charlie Chaplin (1889–1977) was a beloved English comedic actor, best known for his "Tramp" roles in a number of silent films in the 1920s. He'd always been interest in performance and comedy, and though born into a poor family in London, he began performing in music halls at a young age. When he was nineteen, he was discovered by Fred Karno, a music hall actor and slapstick comedy specialist. Karno ended up taking Chaplin to America in 1914, where a new industry, film-making, was getting started in Los Angeles. Chaplin began to work for Keystone Studios, and his signature look with his bowler hat, cane, and tiny moustache soon became famous.

He became a major star of silent movies in the 1920s, appearing in films such as *The Kid* (1921), *A Woman of Paris* (1923), *The Gold Rush* (1925), and *The Circus* (1928). He also directed, produced, wrote, and even composed music for his films, which was a level of control undreamed of today! Of course, as silent films gave way to "talkies," Chaplin had a difficult time of things, until he appeared in the talking-film masterpiece, *The Great Dictator,* in 1940. Though it had comic elements, it also strongly condemned Hitler, Mussolini, and fascism in general.

Chaplin's popularity continued to decline, however, and he had troubles with US law, as some were branding him a communist sympathizer in the 1950s, when the witch hunts for suspected American communists were heating up. He left the US and lived out his life in Switzerland. After his death, his body was dug up and stolen by two men trying to ransom it back to his widow, but they were found out and jailed. Just another anecdote to think about.

There is one amusing story from 1920, which might or might not be true, depending on who you believe. By that time, he was riding a wave of popularity, and his signature look was all the rage. Chaplin lookalike contests popped up in various places around the US, and Chaplin once thought it would be fun to secretly enter such a contest. According to an Australian newspaper report, "A competition in Charlie Chaplin impersonations was held in California recently. There was something like 40 competitors, and Charlie Chaplin, as a joke, entered the contest under an assumed name. He impersonated his well-known film self. But he did not win; he was 27th in the competition."

Another version says that he came in twentieth, and that the competition was held in 1921. So, is it true, or just a funny urban legend? We'll probably never know, but the idea of secretly entering such a competition does sound like something Chaplin would have done for laughs. We can only hope it's a true story!

HEDY LAMARR
TOOK IT DOWN TO
THE WIRE(LESS)

Hedy Lamarr (1914–2000) was an Austrian-born actress known for her roles in such movies as *Lady of the Tropics* (1939), *Boom Town* (1940), *H.M. Pulham, Esq.* (1941), *White Cargo* (1942), and her best-known film, Cecil B. DeMille's *Samson and Delilah* (1949). She had managed to escape Nazi Austria and make her way to Hollywood, where she enjoyed a successful career until

1958. She tried to make a comeback in the 1960s, but failed and ended up living her later years in seclusion.

While her acting career was impressive, she had a lifelong interest in inventions, and made another contribution to the world, without which our technology might be very different today. During World War II, she formulated ideas for wireless technology that were later incorporated into Bluetooth, GPS, Wi-Fi, and other technologies. During the war, she learned about the idea that torpedoes could be developed that would be radio controlled. The problem was that such torpedoes might be susceptible to having their guidance systems jammed, thus sending them off course. She and her friend, the pianist George Antheil, started thinking about ways that a signal could be developed to override any such jamming, as you do.

She came up with a design, and Antheil built a practical model of how it might work, using a player piano mechanism. Basically, they created a way for the guidance transmitter and the receiver to jump to different frequencies simultaneously, which would remove the danger that they could be intercepted and controlled remotely by a third party. This idea would become known as "frequency hopping," though it wasn't completely new. Inventors such as Guglielmo Marconi (inventor of the radio) and Nikola Tesla (the eccentric genius) had both written about the idea a few decades earlier.

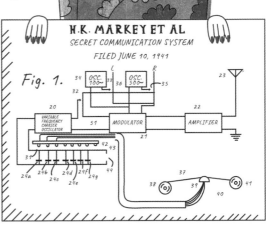

Lamar and Antheil received a patent for their invention in August 1942, but they couldn't interest the US Navy in it because the design was cumbersome (they said), and neither the US nor any other country was using radio-controlled torpedoes at the time. So they probably thought that this technology wasn't worth the time, effort, or investment to test out. That was no doubt disappointing for Lamar and Antheil, but it wasn't the end. By the 1960s, the basic principles of Lamar's design and Antheil's mock-up began to be used in real-life devices. During the Cuban Missile Crisis in 1962, the US blockade ships were all armed with torpedoes using the frequency hopping system. Later, the same ideas would find their way into Bluetooth and GPS as well as some older forms of Wi-Fi.

For their innovations and contributions, both Lamar and Antheil received the Electronic Frontier Foundation Pioneer Award in 1997, and were inducted into the National Inventors Hall of Fame in 2014. It's safe to say that our tech might be different or might not even exist without Lamar's ideas.

AUDREY HEPBURN'S
ANTI-NAZI EFFORTS

Screen legend Audrey Hepburn (1929–93) is beloved by fans worldwide, known not only for her acting but for her stylish fashion sense; she was even inducted into the International Best Dressed List Hall of Fame. Undoubtedly known best for playing Holly Golightly in *Breakfast at Tiffany's*, she also starred in films such as *Roman Holiday*, *War and Peace*, and *My Fair Lady*, among nearly two dozen others. Her talents extended to TV and stage as well. But what most people don't know is that in her youth, she played a role in the Dutch Resistance against the Nazis.

In 1939, she was studying at a school in England. When Britain declared war on Germany, her mother brought her back to Arnhem in the Netherlands, assuming that, as during World War I, the Netherlands would be neutral and Hitler would leave them alone. Of course, this proved to be a mistake. Hepburn's parents supported Hitler. Her mother, Ella van Heemstra, even met him in Munich in 1935, though of course, little Audrey knew nothing about this. She would later feel shame for it.

In Arnhem, she took the name "Edda van Heemstra," to better blend in. Her mother continued to support Germany, even after the Netherlands were invaded, because she assumed it would be over in a matter of weeks. Hepburn later stated that they might have shot themselves if they knew how long the occupation would really be. In any case, the family had to survive, and since Hepburn was already a talented dancer, she performed for German officials.

But in 1942, her uncle, Otto van Limburg Stirum, was executed in retaliation for Resistance sabotage. He had not been involved, but he was made an example of. One of her half-brothers was sent to a labor camp. She also witnessed the beginnings of the Holocaust, saying: "More than once I was at the station seeing trainloads of Jews being transported, seeing all these faces over the top of the wagon. I remember, very sharply, one little boy standing with his parents on the platform, very pale, very blond, wearing a coat that was much too big for him, and he stepped on the train. I was a child observing a child."

All of these horrors seemed to have awoken something in young Hepburn, and she started, in her own way, to do what she could to aid the Dutch Resistance. She organized secret performances to raise money for them, took food and messages to any Allied pilots hiding out nearby, delivered an underground newspaper, and worked in a hospital for a doctor who organized Resistance acts. At one point, her family even hid a British paratrooper, one of the "Red Devils," in their home in 1944, at great personal risk; such actions could result in being shot on the spot if the Germans discovered their activities.

She kept quiet about her efforts after the war, fearful that her family's initial pro-Nazi stance would harm her career, and because she was ashamed of them. She would go on to have a glittering, glamorous career, and her brave stance against Nazi Germany was essentially forgotten until many years later.

CLARK GABLE'S
MOST NOTORIOUS FAN

Clark Gable (1901–60) was the American actor famed for his role as Rhett Butler in *Gone with the Wind*. Over his lifetime, he appeared in no less than sixty-seven films, and had fans across the globe. But one of those fans was someone he definitely didn't want as an admirer: Adolf Hitler.

Hitler loved Gable's movies, and watched them over and over in private screenings. He was such a fan that at one point, he offered $5,000 to anyone who could capture Gable and bring him back to Germany unharmed. Presumably, he would then fawn over him and ask him to make an exclusive movie, or something.

But things were about to change in a way that Hitler never expected. In January of 1942, Gable's wife, Carole Lombard, died when her plane crashed while flying home from a war bonds tour. She was, in fact, the first woman to be killed in an operation related to the war. Gable was devastated and despondent. He wrote to President Roosevelt and asked how he might help out with the war effort. Roosevelt wrote back and said that he should stay in the United States. But Gable needed to do more than just make movies in safety. Ignoring the president's advice, he joined the Army Air Corps and trained as a gunner.

Because the Allies needed a recruitment film to bring in more gunners, Gable was sent to Britain to work on one. He was the perfect choice, a famous movie star who also did exactly the job they needed to portray.

The Germans learned of this, and pompously announced that they would soon be hosting him; perhaps Hitler's dream was about to come true? But Gable was determined and took part in bombing missions over Germany, one of which almost killed him. He was keenly aware of the price on his head, and always feared that he would be taken and forced to participate in Nazi propaganda. Nevertheless, he always escaped being captured. This fact frustrated Hitler immensely. Not only was his dream of meeting his hero shattered, but he couldn't even abduct him and brag about it!

Gable went on to have an illustrious military career during the war, being promoted to the rank of major and earning various medals for his service. On the other side, we all know what happened to Hitler...

LUCILLE BALL
AND *STAR TREK*

Lucille Ball (1911–89) is a beloved television comedian and icon; *I Love Lucy* remains popular with legions of fans to this day. This comedy, in which she costarred with husband Desi Arnaz, ran from 1951 to 1957, and made them both household names. They were successful enough that they even had their own studio, Desilu Productions, which Ball took over on her own after the couple divorced in 1960. This role made her one of the most powerful people (not just women) in Hollywood at the time.

And so it was that a young man named Gene Rodenberry came to her in 1964 with an idea: a science fiction series, *Star Trek*, about a group of people traveling among the stars. Ball liked it and bought it, even though she seems to have misunderstood the idea at first, and thought it was about a group of USO performers traveling in Europe during World War II! Technically, they were "stars" making the "trek" to somewhere.

In any case, Roddenberry was able to explain the actual premise and convince Ball that her studio should fund it. She did, even though some of her board members didn't like the idea and objected to it, thinking it would never sell. Boy, do they look foolish now! The studio produced a pilot, called "The Cage," which failed to attract any takers. That might have been the end of it, but Roddenberry and company went back and retooled things and made a second pilot, again with Ball's blessing and support. Even back then, getting a second chance for a television show was almost unheard of, but Ball really wanted to see *Star Trek* come to life.

This time, a version starring William Shatner made a bigger impression. With Ball's support, NBC picked it up, and the rest, as they say, is history. Though the show only ran for three seasons, *Star Trek* soon became a worldwide phenomenon that remains popular to this day: movies, new TV series, novels, games, toys, you name it, there's some kind of Trek tie-in. And it's all due to the fact that Ball believed in the show and her influential studio backed it.

According to an accountant at Desilu at the time, "If it were not for Lucy, there would be no *Star Trek* today." Nearly sixty years ago, she "beamed up" a genre-defining mega-success.

JACK NICHOLSON'S
SISTER WASN'T
ACTUALLY HIS SISTER

Jack Nicholson is widely regarded as one of the great actors of the twentieth century. A three-time Oscar winner and six-time Golden Globe recipient, he has starred in films ranging from *One Flew Over the Cuckoo's Nest* to *China Town* to *The Shining* to *Batman*, which is about as diverse a collection of movies as one can imagine! His place in cinema history is assured, and his films will continue to be admired for generations to come.

But poor Jack made an unusual discovery in 1974, when *Time* magazine did some digging and found out a bit of unsettling news: the woman that Nicholson had always thought was his older sister was, in fact, his biological mother! June Francis gave birth to Nicholson in 1937 when she was only eighteen years old, having gotten pregnant at seventeen. The situation was made worse by the fact that she wasn't sure who the father was.

She was involved with a showman named Donald Furcillo (known as Donald Rose), but then found out that he was already married. June's mother, Ethel May, threatened Don with legal action if he didn't stay away from June. Don might well have been the father, but June's manager, Eddie King, might have had that honor instead. In any case, this was the kind of scandal that people couldn't deal with in the 1930s, so the family resorted to the only answer they could think of: they simply acted like it didn't exist!

Ethel May agreed to pretend to be Jack's mother, while June agreed to act as his sister. Ethel May's husband John, of course, would take the role of his father. In addition, Jack's aunt, Lorraine, agreed to be another sister. And that's how he grew up, since they never bothered to tell him the truth.

But in 1974, some people at *Time* magazine were doing research for a story and they stumbled onto the rather shocking truth. Both June and Ethel had died by then, so Nicholson never had the chance to talk with them about it. But he seemed to take it all fairly well, saying that it was, "a pretty dramatic event, but it wasn't what I'd call traumatizing... I was pretty well psychologically formed."

Still, learning about one's true family history from a major news magazine is not something that happens every day!

HARRISON FORD
COULD HAVE BEEN
"FORCED" OUT

Harrison Ford is truly a legend in his own time. He has portrayed Han Solo, Indiana Jones, Rick Deckard, Jack Ryan, and many more over a career spanning over fifty years. Some of his roles have become so iconic that it's nearly impossible to see anyone else in them. Indeed, films and shows with younger versions of Han Solo and Indiana Jones, for example, don't always meet with audience approval.

But incredible as it sounds, he was not in the running at first to play Han Solo when George Lucas was casting the first *Star Wars* film back in the mid-70s. Ford had appeared in a minor role in Lucas' previous film, *American Graffiti*, and Lucas was dead-set against using anyone he'd previously worked with for *Star Wars*; he wanted new faces. So a number of different actors were considered for the role of the charming but arrogant Solo, including: Al Pacino, Burt Reynolds, Jack Nicholson, Robert De Niro, Sylvester Stallone, Christopher Walken, Bill Murray, Kurt Russell, Steve Martin, and Chevy Chase, among others. It's mind-blowing to think that one of these guys could have ended up playing one of the greatest science fiction movie roles of all time!

But as luck would have it, Ford was doing some carpentry work at the office of Francis Ford Coppola on the same day that Lucas started holding auditions for Solo there. Lucas came in with Richard Dreyfus, the first actor to audition for the part. Lucas remembered Ford, and ultimately hired him to read lines with those actors who were auditioning. Amazingly, he was taken with Ford's presence and talent and decided to offer the role to him instead, backtracking his commitment to only work with new actors. It was a huge triumph for Ford and would elevate his acting career to superstar status in only a few years.

AUDITION LIST
- AL PACINO
- BURT REYNOLDS
- JACK NICHOLSON
- ROBERT DE NIRO
- SYLVESTER STALLONE
- CHRISTOPHER WALKEN
- BILL MURRAY
- STEVE MARTIN
- CHEVY CHASE

MAYBE: HARRISON FORD?

Though Ford got the coveted job and would end up working with Lucas for years, the two didn't always get along on set. Especially during the *Star Wars* films, he criticized some of the dialogue and Lucas' overall writing (a criticism that other actors have also levelled at Lucas).

Fortunately for Ford, he got to play the final version of Han Solo. One earlier version had him as a green-skinned alien with gills and no nose, while another version imagined him as a big-bearded, swashbuckling pirate! Everyone is happier with how it actually turned out.

WOODY HARRELSON'S
HITMAN DAD

Woody Harrelson got his memorable start in acting as the dim-but-sweet Woody Boyd on the TV sitcom *Cheers*, a role which he played for eight seasons. He would go on to appear in a huge variety of movies and TV shows, everything from *Natural Born Killers* to *The Hunger Games* series, from *True Detective* to *Zombieland*. His fame and acclaim are beyond doubt, but many people don't know the shocking story of his father, Charles Harrelson.

Charles was born in Texas, and in his early days worked in jobs as varied as an encyclopedia salesman and a professional gambler. But as early as 1960, he was already having run-ins with the law, even being convicted of armed robbery. In 1968, he abandoned his wife Diane and their sons Woody, Jordan, and Brett. From then on, his life took a more violent turn. In that same year, he was tried for the murder of a carpet salesman, but the jury acquitted him. He was not so fortunate in 1973, when he was tried and convicted of killing Sam Degelia Jr., a grain dealer in Texas. He was sentenced to fifteen years in prison, but released after five years for good behavior.

That behavior didn't last too long, though, and in 1978, he was caught up in the murder of US District Judge John H. Wood Jr., who was shot dead in San Antonio. Charles was found guilty of the murder, having been paid $250,000 by drug dealer Jamiel Chagra, who apparently was due to go on trial with Wood presiding as the judge. Charles would later say that he didn't commit the murder, but only claimed that he did so he could collect payment from Chagra.

The jury found Charles guilty and sentenced him to two life terms, while those around him received various sentences for conspiracy. Chagra's brother Joe was among them, though in 2003, he recanted his plea confession and claimed that Charles had not assassinated the judge.

Woody had lost all contact with his dad after 1968, but reconnected with him after hearing about the sentence. He often visited him in prison and has never been convinced that he was guilty of the murder.

In an interview with Barbara Walters many years ago, he stated, "I think that it was not a fair trial, especially because the guy who supposedly hired my father to commit the murder was later acquitted on a retrial. I'm not saying my father's a saint, but I think he's innocent of that."

Harrelson also thinks that his dad was actually working with the CIA, though he won't share the details. He tried unsuccessfully to have his father's conviction overturned, and Charles died in prison in 2007 of an apparent heart attack at the age of sixty-eight. If he was innocent, he took that knowledge with him.

CHRISTOPHER WALKEN
IS NOT "LION"
ABOUT HIS MOVIES

Christopher Walken has been entertaining movie audiences with his unique style for decades. It's difficult to know what he'll do next, as he's acted in so many different kinds of films and TV shows (as well as on stage) across numerous genres. He's won an Oscar, a BAFTA Award, and a Screen Actors Guild Award for his efforts. He also has an amazing streak of regularly appearing on both the big and small screens. Between 1975 and 2023, the only years that he didn't appear in a film or a TV show were 1984 and 2010 (and in 1984 he was doing live theater). That's quite a run—one that most other actors would envy! Walken said that he's never really had hobbies, and that acting is his true love. Most of the time when he leaves his home, it's for work.

You would expect someone with the ability to play so many roles to be fairly complex and interesting, but most people don't know that he once had a pretty dangerous job as a teenager: taming lions! There have been rumors that he ran away from home to join a circus (the classic cliché), but Walken says the real story was much less dramatic. He was simply offered a summer job as a trainee lion tamer, saying, "Who's going to turn that down?"

He worked with a lion named Sheba, and talking about his job, he said, "I would come into the cage and wave my whip, and she'd lazily get up and sit like a dog and maybe give a little roar." So it didn't sound like she was interested in being "tamed." The whole thing was just for show, anyway, as he explained: "It was fake. Well, it was fake in the sense that the real lion tamer who owned the small circus… would do this big act with a dozen big cats. Then he would send them all out at the end and just leave this one old girl, and I would come in… She was very sweet."

Walken admits to having a fondness for cats, so perhaps it was only natural that he would give this job a try, despite the potential danger; a "sweet" lion can still get hungry and aggressive! But it wasn't ever going to be enough, since acting was his real love. Happily for fans everywhere, he left the lion behind and went on to bigger (and less life-threatening) things.

TOM HANKS
HAS A TYPE

Tom Hanks is one of the most beloved actors in the world. His string of hits is truly astonishing. He got his start on TV, as many young actors do, but quickly graduated to films, which only got bigger and more celebrated as his career went on. By the 1990s, he was an award-winning mega-star, appearing in films such as *Forrest Gump*, *Apollo 13*, the *Toy Story* films, and *Saving Private Ryan*, among many others. He's especially known for playing everyman roles, down-to-earth characters that audiences can identify with. He has been in comedies, action films, dramas, and animated films, and always brings his unique voice and personality to his work. He's earned the respect of fellow actors and the industry, and remains one of the "good guys" in Hollywood.

He's very picky about roles, only taking those that genuinely interest him and are unusual enough to really stand out. But when he writes back to people about films, business, or almost anything else, he most often likes to do it in an old-fashioned way: by using a typewriter.

Hanks has more than 250 (!) typewriters in his collection, and he has used them all. He says of his collection, "Every [typewriter] is as individual as a set of fingerprints. So, every time you type something on a typewriter, it is a one-of-a-kind work of art."

He told the London Literature Festival in 2017: "What thrills me about type-writers, is that they are meant to do one thing and one thing only and with the tiniest amount of effort, mainte-nance, it will last a thousand years."

In his youth, his first typewriter was a plastic "hunk of junk," but he soon replaced it with a more quality machine. After that, he never looked back, and has been adding to his considerable collection ever since.

He uses typewriters for every-thing from simple letters to more complex works. He describes the feeling: "Everything you type on a typewriter sounds grand, the

words forming in mini-explosions of SHOOK SHOOK SHOOK. A thank-you note resonates with the same heft as a literary masterpiece." The physical sensation is also pleasurable, he explains, and your hands control how loud or quiet each key stroke is.

There is something grounding and wholesome about hearing that this enormously popular movie star prefers to use an antiquated way of communicating, in an age when most people just rattle off texts on their cell phones that are read once and then deleted. A typed letter (like a handwritten one) can become a thing to keep and enjoy. Tom's devotion to typing reminds us to slow down a bit and appreciate things we can actually touch and experience.

ANGELINA JOLIE
ALMOST HAD A DEAD-END JOB

Angelina Jolie is a versatile actress who took the world by storm with a string of hit movies, including *Girl, Interrupted; Lara Croft: Tomb Raider; Mr. & Mrs. Smith; Kung Fu Panda; Maleficent; Eternals;* and many more. She's won an Oscar and three Golden Globes, and has been listed as Hollywood's highest-paid actress on more than one occasion.

She's also well known for her humanitarian work around the world. While filming *Lara Croft* in Cambodia, she became aware of the human rights abuses as a result of war. She would soon begin advocating for refugees around the world, visiting more than thirty countries and speaking with victims about their horrific experiences. She has also campaigned for children's rights, ending sexual violence, and conservation efforts. Her work has earned her much praise and several awards from international organizations.

But if all of this hadn't happened, she had a decidedly different plan: to become a funeral director. "It sounds like this very strange, eccentric, dark thing to do," she explained in an interview with 60 Minutes, "but in fact I lost my grandfather and was very upset with his funeral... How somebody passes and how family deals with this passing and what death is should be addressed in a different way... If this whole acting thing didn't work out that was going to be my path."

So her interest was born out a concern that our rites for honoring the dead in this society aren't as good as they could be, a legitimate criticism of how we think of and react to death. Having seen the plight of many in war-torn regions around the world, she is no stranger to death and its effects on survivors. While she is a skilled actress, she is also a remarkable human being who no doubt would have brought that same care and compassion to funeral work, if that had been her career path. While fans can be grateful for her many movies, they should also be thankful for her efforts to help those in need around the world.

OTHER ENTERTAINERS

MARIE-MADELEINE GUIMARD'S
SECRET SURVIVAL DURING THE FRENCH REVOLUTION

Marie-Madeleine Guimard (1743–1816) was a famed ballet dancer during the reign of the soon-to-be-headless Louis XVI. She was not only a professional ballet dancer, but also a courtesan, a producer of live sex shows, and a benefactor to the poor and needy.

Ballerinas at the time often moonlighted as courtesans (whether by choice or by necessity) and Guimard made a good deal of money in her work. In 1768, she came up with the idea of putting on pornographic ballets and other stage shows for rich and discrete audiences. Such shows were pretty popular in pre-revolutionary France, and a lot of them were staged and managed by women. They didn't present any dangerous political ideas (such as, you know, cutting off a king's head), so the authorities tended to ignore them.

Guimard did very well for herself, but the times were changing, and pretty soon, she risked being a target of those folks who would be eager to guillotine anyone and everyone associated with the upper classes, including those that served them. By 1785, she had to close down her operations and think about her own safety. And she had spent a lot of money on these lavish adult entertainments and was facing financial troubles. So she sold her properties and tried to wait things out. One of her sponsors lost his head, as did the father of her children.

You might think that she would try to escape Paris and France in general, but that was risky at best, as revolutionaries patrolled everywhere, looking for those exact kinds of people. So, she decided to hide out in an attic in a house in Montmartre, which was up on a steep hill in Paris. It was steep enough, in fact, that guards and soldiers couldn't be bothered to march up it to look for enemies of the state. Too bad nobody ever told Louis XVI and Marie Antoinette about this!

So what did she do during those dangerous years, besides keep her head down, but still attached to her body? She put on marionette sex shows and continued to make money. Seriously. Her porn puppets were all the (quiet) rage, since people apparently still wanted naughty entertainments, even as their friends were losing their heads. Never underestimate the power of lewd entertainment!

Despite all the daily dangers in Paris, and the extra risks she took in staging her saucy string-puppet shows, Guimard survived the French Revolution and lived until 1816, well into her seventies.

P.T. BARNUM'S
APPALLING BEHAVIOR
AND OUTRAGEOUS LIES

P.T. Barnum (1810–91) famously said, "There's a sucker born every minute," except that he didn't actually say it, so the suckers are the ones who believe him. But if he had said it, he would probably have been referring to everyone around him, because boy could he tell some whoppers! Barnum, of course, was a famous showman and circus promoter (teaming up with James Bailey to create the so-called "Greatest Show on Earth"), but the circus part of his long career came later, when he was about sixty years old.

He began his career on a much darker note, by ruthlessly abusing an old African American woman so that he could make money off of her. When he was twenty-five, he met Joice Heth, an elderly slave who some said was George Washington's 161–year-old nurse. It was ridiculous, of course—she was actually about eighty—but Barnum was already scheming about how he could make a profit off of the myth. He arranged to "lease" Heth (whatever that means!), since buying slaves was already illegal in New York. He then took her out on the show circuit, using the same nonsense story about her being baby George's nurse. The skeptical public wasn't buying it, of course, so Barnum had to take a different angle on things to get the cash flowing in.

He decided that she looked too healthy, and he wanted her to be thinner. So he put her on a restricted diet of whiskey and eggs. He then decided that a 161–year-old woman probably would have few, if any, teeth. He asked her if he could pull her teeth out and she, of course, said "no way." So he got her really drunk on whiskey and did it anyway. Yeah, he was a real scumbag. His alterations worked, and people started flocking to see Heth, and of course, she didn't get a single penny of the money, even though he assured audiences in the slave free North that money was going to help her still-enslaved family in the south. He pretty much just said what he thought anyone would want to hear. But at some point, the novelty of George Washington's nurse wore off, and he had to think of a new angle, so he started presenting her as an automaton, basically a robot, made up of whale bones, rubber, and clock springs. Seriously.

Poor Heth died less than a year after this whole mess started, but even that didn't deter Barnum. He scheduled a public autopsy of her body and charged circus visitors fifty cents each for admission to watch. This hideous behavior was just the beginning of a lifetime of cons and lies that Barnum pulled off to make himself rich. He should have been in prison, but he went from one success to another, always looking for the next big thing that would wow audiences, no matter how outrageous.

He once tried to buy the ruins of Pompeii (presumably to turn them into a spectacle), as well as the house where Shakespeare was born in

Stratford-upon-Avon, but thankfully both the Italian and British governments told him to get lost. Incredibly, he often proclaimed that he hated liars who tried to take advantage of people. This from a man who once sewed part of a monkey corpse to a dead fish and charged admission to see a "mermaid."

MATA HARI'S
MISSING HEAD

Mata Hari (1876–1917) is best known as a dancer and spy, who worked during World War I, and was caught and executed. And that's all true, but there's more to the story, and to what happened to her after her execution. She was born Margaretha Geertruida Zelle in 1878 in the Netherlands, and lived a pretty privileged life until her father went bankrupt and left her mother when she was about eleven years old.

She managed to make do for a few years, and eventually married an army captain named Rudolph MacLeod. He was about twenty years older than her, and soon they packed up and moved to Java, in the Dutch East Indies. They had two children, but the marriage was unhappy, and began to fall apart. At the same time, Margaretha started taking dance lessons, learning a form called Gandrung, an Indonesian courtship dance that seems to have been done in devotion to the goddess of rice. She chose the stage name "Mata Hari," which means "Eye of the Dawn" in the Malay language.

Tragedy soon struck when her son died in 1899 (he might even have been poisoned). She returned to Europe and divorced MacLeod, though he made her life miserable in revenge. She sought refuge in Paris, and became something of a sensation as the "exotic" dancer, Mata Hari. She lied about her background, claiming to be the daughter of a Hindu priest, among other things.

As World War I began, she fell in love with a Russian officer, who was later wounded. She wanted to visit him in his hospital in northeastern France, but needed special permission to go. Georges Ladoux, head of French intelligence, wanted her to spy when she went there, since she was Dutch, and the Dutch were officially neutral in the war. She agreed, but things went wrong pretty quickly, and she traveled to both Britain and France before ending up back in Paris and being accused of spying on the Allies. It's possible that Ladoux set her up. In any case, she was sentenced to be executed by firing squad, a sad ending for a woman who was pretty obviously wronged by those around her.

But it got even worse after her death, if you can imagine that. Since no one would claim her body, her head was removed and sent to the Museum of Anatomy in Paris. And that wasn't even the worst thing. In 2000, it was discovered that her head had gone missing in the 1950s, and no one had noticed! Who took her head and why? Where is it now? Does someone still have it? No one knows the answers to these chilling questions!

JOSEPHINE BAKER'S
DOUBLE LIFE DURING
WORLD WAR II

Josephine Baker (1906–75) was a legendary singer, dancer, and actress, who made quite the splash in Paris during the years leading up to World War II. She was known for her skimpy banana skirt and her pet cheetah, among other things. She delighted audiences on stage at the Folies Bergère in Paris, and was the first Black woman to star in a major motion picture: the silent film, *Siren of the Tropics*. You might be surprised that such a high-profile person would also work as a spy, but that's just what she did.

The granddaughter of a slave, Baker was born in Arkansas and grew up in St. Louis. She tried to have a performer's life in New York, but decided to go to Paris in 1925, feeling that she might face less racism and resistance there; she was right. Paris warmly embraced her and she was the talk of the town during the Roaring 20s. Her fame continued through the troubled years of the 1930s, as the winds of war again stirred. And it was this fame that made her potentially useful as Hitler's assault on Europe began in earnest.

Jacques Abtey, a French intelligence officer, recruited her after she convinced him of her loyalty to France and hatred of the Nazis. Baker had earned a pilot's license in 1936, and between 1939 and 1940, she flew her own airplane to help deliver supplies to refugees fleeing from the Nazi onslaught. Because of her fame, she'd made friends with various Italian diplomats and her first official mission was to determine if Mussolini was going to throw his hat in with Hitler (he did). She also used her friendship with the wife of the Japanese ambassador to discover that Japan was also ready to enter the war.

When Paris fell to the Nazis, she retreated to her chateau, Milandes, acting neutral, but continued to work in secret to help stock weapons, give the Resistance a place to hide, and shelter Jewish refugees. She married a Jewish businessman, which provoked the suspicions of Hermann Göring. He invited her to a dinner in Paris, and intended to poison her with cyanide in her fish. She was tipped off and tried to avoid eating the deadly food, but he forced her to at gunpoint. She went to a bathroom and escaped out a laundry shoot, where fellow Resistance members sped her away to a doctor to have her stomach pumped. She survived!

She went on tour outside of France, but worked with Abtey to smuggle information to the Allies via Portugal to London. When she performed, she hid information about German troop movements in her sheet music, and even sewed messages and photos into her underwear and dresses.

Knowing she was no longer safe in France, she fled to Algeria, and continued to work with Abtey to gather information about troop movements and defenses ahead of Operation Torch, the Allies' invasion of North Africa in November, 1942. She became seriously ill, but recovered and continued to perform. Her only requirement for the troops seeing her was that they not be segregated.

After the war, she returned to her home in France, and received many awards. General Charles de Gaulle named her a Chevalier of the *Légion d'honneur*, and the French hailed her as a war hero. She happily took up her entertainment life again, having done more than her part to help turn back the fascist onslaught.

ROBERT RIPLEY
AND THE MAN BEHIND THE SCENES OF *BELIEVE IT OR NOT*

Ripley's Believe It or Not is a famous and beloved institution of collected unusual and sometimes plain bizarre facts. These have been presented to the public through Ripley's cartoons, as well as books, photos, and later the "Odditoriums," or museums; there are thirty-two of these around the world. Ripley's attractions are a highlight of many a childhood!

Born in Santa Rosa, California (north of San Francisco), Robert Ripley (1890–1949) was a shy boy who entertained himself by drawing. Illustration became his passion, and by the age of sixteen, he was already working as a sports cartoonist for various newspapers. In those days, sports photography was in its infancy, so papers relied on illustrators to draw the athletes instead. At the same time, he had an insatiable curiosity about the world and all of its weird and wonderful facts, and he wanted to bring those to his readers. He had a cartoon strip, *Champs and Chumps*, for the New York Globe, but as he began to add non-sports facts to it, he changed the name to the now-famous *Believe It or Not*.

He embarked on a trip around the world in 1922 and recorded his findings in his journal, which he later published. Knowing that he wouldn't have the time to do all the research himself, and also wanting to make sure that his stories were accurate, he hired a researcher, Norbert Pearlroth, who came from Poland. He was fluent in fourteen (!) languages, and Ripley knew that he would be the perfect man for the job, since he could read stories from around the world.

He was Ripley's only researcher, and was the hidden man behind the phenomenon. He would often work ten hours a day, six days a week, with afternoons mostly spent in the main branch of the New York Public library. While Ripley did indeed travel the world (he visited more than 200 countries), Pearlroth's son would later say that much of Ripley's information "was really found on 42nd Street and Fifth Avenue at the Main Library." The *Believe It or Not* organization received up to 3,000 letters a week from fans, and Pearlroth did his best to answer them. Many of these were the time's equivalent of the "well actually" responses on social

NY PUBLIC LIBRARY
BELIEVE IT OR NOT!

media, with readers trying to point out how he was wrong, but Pearlroth insisted that he always did his homework, and that his facts were accurate.

Much of his life was spent there, except the occasional times when he would accompany Ripley on a trip somewhere. After Ripley died in 1949, Pearlroth continued his work for the strip until 1975, with twenty-four new facts each week. He was the often-forgotten hero behind the phenomenon.

WALT DISNEY'S
GIFT TO HIS HOUSEKEEPER

Walt Disney (1901–66) will live forever in the hearts of countless children and adults for his incredible creations, from Mickey Mouse to films like *Snow White* and *Cinderella*, from merchandise to Disneyland and the other themes parks that bear his name. The Disney corporation itself is a formidable entity, one of the most powerful entertainment companies in the world, to the delight of some and the anger and worry of others; having both Marvel and Star Wars under one roof is an amazing achievement to some and too much power to others.

There have been a few strange stories about Walt over the years, like that his body (or even just his head) is cryogenically frozen in a vault underneath Disneyland (spoiler alert: it's not), but there is one verifiable story about him that deserves to be told.

Disney's housekeeper, Thelma Howard, had come from a difficult background (having lost her mother and sister as a young child), and though she had training as a stenographer, she took up housekeeping. She was hired by Disney as a live-in housekeeper in 1951 for his, shall we say, large home in Los Angeles. It had eight bedrooms, seventeen bathrooms, a putting green, a tennis court, a gym, a swimming pool, etc. All the things a Hollywood superstar needed, apparently. But not only did Thelma manage it all, she became a close family friend and helped to raise his daughters, Sharon and Diane. Disney was so impressed by her that he once called her the "real-life Mary Poppins." She became a valued member of the family in her own right and had room and board as part of her salary—not a bad deal.

But in addition, Disney also gave her shares of Disney company stock every year as a Christmas gift. Howard wisely never sold them (and sometimes bought extra on her own), and of course over time, they grew in value to a tremendous amount as the company's value only continued to climb. She established the Thelma Pearl Howard Foundation to help fund community arts projects for Los Angeles children up through eighth grade. And by the early 1990s, her shares were worth over $9 million! It's estimated that they would be worth up to $85 million now. In any case, the money went to both her son and her foundation, a lovely way of giving back something to the community, and Walt helped make it possible when he realized how valuable she was to him and his family.

THE 1919 WORLD SERIES
SCANDAL

Baseball has long been the "great American pastime," but by the early twentieth century, it was already a big enough business that rot had started to creep in. As so often happens, money has the potential to taint everything, and the infamous 1919 World Series proves that well enough. Gambling on sports matches was already a big deal in those days, and with the upcoming World Series (a best-of-nine games affair back then), some bookies and pros started to see a way that they could make a killing.

The Chicago White Sox were the favorites to win the series against the Cincinnati Reds, by a pretty large margin. But as the first game unfolded, it was obvious that something seemed more than a bit off. White Sox pitcher Eddie Cicotte "accidentally" hit a batter, and after that made a string of atypical mistakes. He was not the type to crack under the pressure of being in a championship game, and other members of the team also underperformed. At the end of the game, the Reds had trounced the White Sox by a score of 9–1, which was unexpected, to say the least. Even the *New York Times* declared, "Never before in the history of America's biggest baseball spectacle has a pennant-winning club received such a disastrous drubbing in an opening game."

But it only got worse. The White Sox lost the second game, though this time only by 4–2. Again, there were some very strange mistakes, and people began to wonder what was up. There were rumors that several White Sox players were on the take and were being offered money to throw the series. Also, it was said that some high-rolling gamblers were betting on the Reds, against the odds, and people began to wonder if at least some of the White Sox's players had been bribed to deliberately lose.

By the fifth game, the White Sox were behind 4–1, and on the verge of losing the championship. But then something happened, and they sprang to life.

They beat the Reds in the next two games, and put themselves right back into contention for the title. They looked like their old selves again. But then, they lost once more (10–5) and thus the title went to the Reds.

So what happened? It would later emerge that several White Sox players were indeed approached, probably by organized crime, to throw the series in exchange for at least $100,000, about $1.5 million in modern value. For the poorly-paid players, it must have been too good to be true. Apparently, these players were supposed to receive their money in $20,000 increments, one after each lost game, but of course, those making the offer hadn't produced all the money. The angry players decided to back out and go back to winning (hence games six and seven). But then, they lost again. Were they threatened for going back on their end of the bargain? Quite possibly.

The following year, suspicions arose about gambling in baseball, and a grand jury investigated the World Series. A gambler named Bill Maharg came forward and confessed to his involvement. Soon, various White Sox players also testified that they had been paid to throw the series. They went to trial, charged with conspiracy, but all of the paperwork related to their guilt mysteriously "disappeared," most likely at the behest of the mob. The prosecution didn't have enough to convict and the players were acquitted, though the new commissioner, Kenesaw Mountain Landis, banned them for life from playing professional baseball.

The 1919 World Series was an ugly scandal that still ranks as a low point in the history of the sport.

THAT TIME TEENAGER
JACKIE MITCHELL
(MAYBE) STRUCK OUT THE BABE

On April 2, 1931, teenage girl and left-handed baseball pitcher Jackie Mitchell (1913–87) stepped onto the pitcher's mound at an exhibition game against the mighty New York Yankees, featuring such batting legends as Babe Ruth and Lou Gehrig. Jackie played for a Tennessee minor-league team, the Lookouts, whose manager, Joe Engel, had managed to swing (pun intended) two exhibition games against the Yankees, of all teams. It was great publicity for Chattanooga, and crowds turned out in droves. Engel had only signed Mitchell a week before, and this was probably one of the first, if not *the* first, professional baseball contract offered to a woman.

Of course, the sexist press laughed at the prospect of a young woman going up against the likes of Ruth and Gehrig. And it probably was the novelty of the idea that made over 4,000 people turn out to see the game. The legendary Babe Ruth was up first. The first pitch was a ball, but Babe swung on the next... and missed. He also missed the next pitch and asked the umpire to inspect the baseball, assuming there might have been something funny about it. But it was fine and Mitchell delivered another pitch, and another strike. Babe actually threw down his bat in disgust and stormed off.

Next up was the equally impressive Gehrig. Three pitches, three strikes, and he was out. The crowd was astonished. Who was this amazing young lady who could destroy two of the greatest batters in the game so easily?

She walked the next batter and then the manager pulled her from the game. Her achievement made headlines the following day, but of course, some people were skeptical.

Did Mitchell really strike out these two greats, or did they swing and miss on purpose to try to make a good show of it? The game was originally intended to be played on April 1, which might indicate that the whole thing was a fake. But another player for the Yankees at the time said that their manager was competitive and had integrity, and wouldn't have instructed the players to deliberately throw the game. It's possible that Ruth and Gehrig privately agreed to strike out, but they never admitted to this. Mitchell always believed that she'd really struck out both of them.

Modern historians are mixed in their opinions. Some think it's likely that Ruth and Gehrig blew it on purpose, while others point out that being left-handed gives the pitcher an advantage over batters not familiar with them. The grainy film footage that survives is not conclusive. Some historians have suggested that the idea of both batters deliberately missing was just an excuse invented by the sexist press and sports community of the time.

We'll probably never know for sure, but Mitchell was undoubtedly a good pitcher and her appearance on the mound against two of baseball's greatest hitters definitely got a lot of people talking!

L.W. WRIGHT,
THE MYSTERIOUS
NON-NASCAR DRIVER

In April of 1982, an announcement appeared about a new driver for the upcoming Winston 500 at Talladega Superspeedway, one of NASCAR's most prestigious racing events. This driver was named L.W. Wright and he had an impressive record, as well as some big sponsors. He had forty-three Busch Grand National Series starts, and sponsorship from country music legends Merle Haggard, T.G. Sheppard, and Waylon Jennings; his team was called Music City racing. Wright submitted the required entrance fees and was allowed to participate, even though there seemed to be something off about the whole thing.

Wright purchased an expensive car (about $20,000) and all of the extras, including racing jackets; everything was ready for him to take part in the race. But soon, more problems showed up. T.G. Sheppard came forward to say that he had never even heard of Wright, and so was certainly not sponsoring his race. Wright was forced to admit that the announcement about Sheppard's sponsorship was "premature," and that he'd never actually participated in a Grand National Race before. He also didn't seem to know much about racing in general. It was obvious that something was very wrong, and Wright even crashed during a practice run, but was able to get his car fixed in time. During the actual race, he couldn't maintain his speed and ended up finishing thirty-ninth out of forty.

It should have been an embarrassing end for an obvious fraud, but then things got weirder. Wright abandoned the car and disappeared after the race. And soon, his checks for the car and other expenses bounced, too. And that was the end of it. Wright just totally disappeared for forty years, even though NASCAR obtained an arrest warrant and hired private investigators. The story delighted conspiracy theorists and amateur sleuths, but no one could find out where Wright had gone.

Until April of 2022. Rick Houston, a motor racing reporter, was finally able to locate and identify Wright, who agreed to an interview at an "undisclosed location." Wright admitted that he did run the race and left afterward, but denied doing anything else wrong. His health seemed to be poor, and perhaps he just wanted to get some things off his chest in old age. But it seems that, at the very least, Houston had solved one of motor racing's biggest modern mysteries.

So who was Wright? A con man? A dangerous criminal? Or maybe he was just a guy who wanted to see if he could get away with pulling an outrageous stunt? If so, it worked, and he eluded capture for more than four decades.

MUHAMMAD ALI'S
HERITAGE AND CONTROVERSIAL OPINIONS

Muhammad Ali (1942–2016) was, without a doubt, the greatest boxer of the twentieth century, a sports legend who could "float like a butterfly, sting like a bee" and leave his opponents on the boxing ring floor. While his public life is well known, here are some interesting facts about him that reveal an unusual history and background:

- He wasn't born Muhammad Ali, which was a name that Elijah Muhammad of the Nation of Islam gave to him in the 1960s. His birth name was Cassius Marcellus Clay. The significance of the name is that there was a Cassius Marcellus Clay before him, a white southern politician and abolitionist (1810–1903) who was strongly opposed to slavery. He had inherited about forty slaves from his father and freed all of them. He helped to found the new Republican party in Kentucky and later worked with President Lincoln on abolitionist goals. Lincoln also appointed him as the US minister to Russia, and he was able to help gain Russia's support for the Union during the American Civil War.

- It wasn't just Ali's birth name that hinted at connections to the wider world. He was also descended on his mother's side from an Irish immigrant named Abe Grady, who was his great-grandfather. Grady had emigrated from Ireland and settled in Kentucky in the 1860s, after the Civil War. Grady married a free Black woman, herself the daughter of freed slaves. Their granddaughter, Odessa Lee Grady, would marry another Cassius Clay in 1942, and the two would have the son who received his father's name and would go on to be world-famous. Ali would later visit County Clare in Ireland, where his ancestor had come from. He was mobbed by fans eager to see him and who were delighted that they could claim this one part of him as their own.

- More controversially, Ali, as a convert to Islam, declared himself to be a conscientious objector on religious grounds to the Vietnam war, and refused to be conscripted. He famously stated: "Why should they ask me to put on a uniform and go ten thousand miles from home and drop bombs and bullets on brown people in Vietnam while so-called Negro people in Louisville are treated like dogs and denied simple human rights." He was arrested on a felony charge of refusing the draft. He was tried and found guilty, though he was not jailed. In 1971, the Supreme Court heard the case and unanimously overturned Ali's conviction, not on moral grounds, but because the military appeal board had not given a good reason for the denial of a conscientious objector exemption for Ali. He was freed on a legal technicality, and became an increasingly vocal opponent of the Vietnam war, making him hugely popular with other protestors and the counterculture generation.

HATSHEPSUT:
EGYPT'S REMARKABLE
FEMALE PHARAOH

Ancient Egypt immediately conjures up images of pyramids and the Great Sphinx of Giza in most people's minds, but thanks to the fame of King Tut's treasures, even the everyday person on the street probably has some sense of what the pharaohs looked like, with their striped headdresses and long, pointy beards. And of course, they were all men, right? Okay, there was Cleopatra, but she reigned as a queen at the end of Egypt's glory, when Rome was overwhelming the country. And yet, there was an amazing woman who reigned not as a queen of Egypt, but as its pharaoh in her own right, over 1,400 years before Cleopatra lived. Her name was Hatshepsut, and her story is pretty amazing.

She was born sometime between 1504 and 1507 BCE, and reigned from 1479 BCE until her death in 1458 in her early fifties. She was the daughter of Pharaoh Thutmose I, but he died without having any sons, a disaster for the (admittedly sexist) royal line. So Hatshepsut stepped up and did her duty, marrying her half-brother, Thutmose (Thutmose's son by a different, "secondary" wife), to help him secure his claim to be the next pharaoh. Yes, this gives off "ick" vibes, but it was pretty common among royal families back then. He ascended to the throne as Thutmose II, and she became queen at about the age of twelve. More ick.

Anyway, Thutmose II was possibly rather weak and sickly, and he and Hatshepsut failed to have a son, though he did have a son by one of his own "secondary" wives, a boy confusingly also named Thutmose. When Thutmose II died, Hatshepsut assumed the title of Regent to govern Egypt until the infant Thutmose III came of age. Early Egyptologists claimed that she selfishly wanted more, and seized the throne away from young Thutmose III when he was about seven, proclaiming herself pharaoh. Of course, to these Victorian gentlemen, this was horrible and utterly distasteful.

But more recent research suggests that she stepped in to save the throne from political infighting and shore up the boy's claim. Thutmose III was never under arrest, and he continued his education and training as planned. But Hatshepsut reinvented herself and began to have images of herself made showing her as strong and powerful, and yes, wearing the long, false beard of the pharaoh. She renamed herself Maatkare—Maat (the goddess of truth) is the life force of Re (the sun god)—and began a program of building and public works, including her own temple at Deir el-Bahri across the Nile from Thebes. The temple included at least 100 statues of her as a masculine pharaoh, designed to show off her power to visitors and impress them. It worked.

In addition to numerous building projects, she also re-established old trade routes to improve trade and bring new wealth into Egypt. She organized diplomatic missions in various regions, and possibly led military ventures into Nubia and perhaps Canaan, though her reign was mostly peaceful.

After her death, many of her monuments and statues were defaced and destroyed. Scholars long thought that this destruction was simply Thutmose III taking revenge on her for keeping him from the throne, but new research shows that the vandalism probably happened toward the end of his reign, and was probably done to "prove" that the throne had passed directly to him from his father. In any case, Hatshepsut was largely forgotten in the centuries that followed, even though her reign brought peace and prosperity to a kingdom that desperately needed it. Egypt would not have another female ruler like her until Cleopatra.

JULIUS CAESAR
WAS KIDNAPPED BY PIRATES

Caesar (100–44 BCE) is famous for a lot of things: his brilliance as a military leader, the conquest of Gaul, becoming leader of Rome, being declared dictator for life of Rome, and ending up on the wrong end of several pointy blades because of it. The very word "Caesar" became synonymous with being a ruler, and many later leaders would style themselves as "Caesars" long after the Western Roman Empire had crumbled into dust; words like "Kaiser" and "Tsar" are two of the best examples.

Among the many wild and crazy adventures that Caesar had, one of the more unusual was his being kidnapped by pirates when he was twenty-five. In 75 BCE, as he sailed across the Aegean Sea, he was kidnapped by Cilician pirates, who were known for their ruthlessness and ferocity. The young Caesar should have been afraid, but instead, he just ended up annoying them!

They told him that they were ransoming him for the price of twenty talents, or a little over half a ton of silver. He laughed at them and told them they had no idea who they'd captured, but not as a threat. No, he told them this because he said they should increase the ransom to *fifty* talents! Needless to say, the pirates were more than a little confused about this, but Caesar insisted and sent some of his subordinates off to collect the ransom, which would take over a month to gather.

In the meantime, he set about being pretty insufferable to his captors, acting like they were not holding him at all. He would tell them to be quiet when he wanted to sleep, and spent time writing and reciting poetry and speeches, which he made them listen to. He even participated in their training exercises and began to act like their leader. As a result, the pirates actually grew to like him, and let him have freedom to roam the ship and their island base. He told them that after he was released, he would come back and take his revenge on them, and they mostly just laughed, thinking him to be joking.

The ransom money came through, and the delighted pirates took it and released him. Some were probably even sorry to see him go. But Caesar hadn't forgotten, and intended to make good on his threat. He put together a small fleet and sailed back to the island. The pirates and the silver were still there; they'd obviously not taken him seriously. He captured them, took back the ransom, and had them delivered to a prison in the city of Pergamon. He then met with the proconsul of Asia, Marcus Junius, and asked that the pirates be crucified. Junius refused, wanting to sell them as slaves instead. Profit before execution.

But Caesar was undeterred. He went back to the prison and ordered that they be executed. The pirates were all strung up and crucified, but he showed some "mercy" by slitting their throats first, perhaps as a gesture to thank them for their hospitality!

BOUDICCA:
AN EARLY BRITISH BADASS!

Under the emperor Claudius, the Romans finally succeeded in invading and starting to occupy Britain in 43 CE. They'd had their eyes on the island for over a century, ever since Julius Caesar had thought about it but given up. The Romans did what they usually did: occupy with the idea of bringing "peace," but then brutally crush any opposition. They used this same strategy, but they were about to get a very painful pushback that would be remembered in Britain ever after.

A woman named Boudicca (30–60/61 CE) was queen of the Iceni, a Celtic tribe that lived north of what is now London. In the year 60 CE, her husband, King Prasutagus, died without a male heir. He'd left part of his wealth to Boudicca and their daughters, but another part to the Emperor Nero, as a show of friendship to continue their good relations. Of course, this isn't what happened. The Romans confiscated their lands; they had Boudicca whipped and her daughters violated. While the Romans thought they'd beaten the Iceni into submission, they were about to learn otherwise, and very violently.

Boudicca set about taking her revenge almost right away and brought other fed-up Celtic tribes together as a unified force to fight back. When they learned that the Roman general Paulinus was away in another part of the island, they went on the attack. Boudicca, with an army of thousands, met the Ninth Roman legion and destroyed it. Celts were known as fearless fighters, and this battle certainly proved it! Boudicca led the army on to Camulodunum (modern-day Colchester) and destroyed it, massacring the Romans and pro-Roman British inside. They then moved on to London and burned it to the ground, before also destroying Verulamium (modern-day St. Albans), probably killing up to 80,000 people in all of these victories.

Of course, the Romans were in full-on panic mode, and Paulinus had to rush back from a campaign in what is now north Wales to try to meet Boudicca's forces. The two armies met north of London, but this time Boudicca and the Celts were outmatched by the well-trained and disciplined Roman troops. Boudicca was defeated, and she and her daughters might have taken their own lives to avoid capture.

The Romans won the day and went on to remain in Britain for another 300 years, but they never forgot the humiliation and learned not to be so overconfident in the future. Boudicca and her people became symbols of freedom and the fight against oppression, and she is still remembered and honored today.

THEODORA:
FROM ACTRESS TO EMPRESS

Theodora (c. 497/500–548) was empress of the Byzantine Empire from 527 to 548. Her story is improbable, to say the least. Her father was a bear trainer for the Hippodrome games, and in time, she probably followed in her mother's footsteps, becoming an actress, an entertainer, and later on, a courtesan who was in high demand for clients across all ranks of society, though she was known to banish low-paying clients in favor of wealthier ones. She was also said to perform lewd acts on stage for those willing to pay to see them.

The only problem with this version of her life is that it was written by the sixth-century Byzantine historian, Procopius of Caesarea, who, shall we say, was not fond of her. His account of her is probably mostly a gossip-filled hit piece, since he was likely outraged that someone common born achieved what she did. And what did she do? She ascended through the ranks of power in a way that most could only dream of.

Whatever her background, she became a companion to a Syrian politician named Hecebolus and accompanied him to Libya. But the relationship soured and she left to go to Alexandria in Egypt, where she converted to a form of Christianity called Miaphysitism (which holds that Christ has only one nature, divine and human). From there, she traveled to Antioch and probably met representatives of Justinian, the son of Emperor Justin I. The two met and he was immediately taken with her, but he wasn't allowed to marry her because she was born as a commoner, and worse, had been an actress, which, in most minds, was synonymous with being a prostitute. No problem. His father, the emperor, amended an existing law to say that someone of higher rank could indeed marry an actress if the emperor gave his permission. How convenient! Justinian's mother, Empress Lupicina Euphemia, opposed the match, but after her death, there were no further objections.

As a result, Justinian and Theodora were married in 525, and after Justin's death in 527, Justinian and Theodora were crowned as emperor and empress. Justinian insisted that she be crowned empress in her own right. It was an astonishing rags-to-riches story. But Theodora was no ornament. She was deeply involved in politics, attending Justinian's councils and advising him. He even called her his "partner in [his] deliberations." And of course, a lot of men, including Procopius, resented that. Justinian and Theodora oversaw a number of building projects and reforms, including expanding some rights for women. Their greatest legacy was the construction of Hagia Sophia, the monumental cathedral at the heart of the city of Constantinople that still stands proudly over the skyline of Istanbul, 1,500 years later.

Theodora died many years before Justinian, and while the two differed on their interpretations of Christianity, she was later made a saint in both the Eastern Orthodox Church and the Oriental Orthodox Church. Not bad for a woman whose father had trained bears!

ÆTHELFLÆD,
LADY OF THE MERCIANS

Æthelflæd (c. 870–918) was the oldest daughter of King Alfred the Great. She has recently become more well-known thanks to the hit TV series, *The Last Kingdom*. Her father fought against the Danish/Viking forces in the late ninth century, forces which threatened to overwhelm all of England and bring it completely under Danish control. But Alfred held out and managed to fight back, winning freedom for his kingdom of Wessex and for the neighboring land of Mercia. After taking London back in the year 886, he offered the city back to Mercia (who had held it before the Danish occupation) as a token of their alliance.

But Alfred wanted Mercia to recognize Wessex as the "superior" nation in the relationship, and he wanted Mercia's leader, Æthelred, to marry Æthelflæd. Unfortunately, royal women usually didn't have much say in who they married, and she was only sixteen at the time. Alfred wanted to know what was happening in the Mercian court, and having his daughter there was a perfect way to do it.

But Æthelflæd wasn't going to be some quiet little queen doing her husband's bidding. She had an interest in battle strategies and was soon advising her husband on how best to kick out the Danes along Mercia's borders. One time, some Danes were harassing the city of Chester, near the border of Wales. Æthelflæd came to the city with an army and, after pretending to be defeated by them, drew them into the city itself, where the Danes were ambushed and wiped out.

Æthelred died in 911 after a long illness and Æthelflæd became the ruler of Mercia; she was now a queen in all but name. She worked with her brother Edward, Alfred's son and now king of Wessex, and they secured more lands and even turned their attention to trying to unite all of England. Æthelflæd held the title of "Lady of the Mercians" and seemed to have been beloved by her people, in a time when no woman was supposed to have that kind of power. She honored the agreement between Wessex and Mercia, taking a subservient role to Wessex, which no doubt fed Edward's ego!

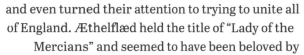

Sadly, she only reigned for seven years before dying in her early forties in 918. We don't know the cause, but death could come pretty quickly and unexpectedly in those days, so it could have been anything from an infected cut to a bad cold, or something much more serious.

In any case, she became a legend in her own time, and still ranks as possibly the most impressive and important woman of the Anglo-Saxon centuries.

ROXELANA:
ONE OF HISTORY'S MOST POWERFUL WOMEN

Hurrem Sultan, also known as Roxelana (c. 1504–58), like Theodora, lived an improbable rags-to-rich life, rising from the status of slave to become the most important woman in the Ottoman Empire. She was born in what is now Rohatyn, in western Ukraine, then a part of the Kingdom of Poland, known to its inhabitants as Ruthenia. Her father was a Ruthenian Orthodox priest. Her actual birth name is unknown, though it might have been Aleksandra or Anastasia. "Hurrem" means "the joyful one" in Persian, while Roxelana comes from the Turkish word *roksolanes*, a word for young women in certain Eastern European regions that the Ottomans took as slaves. In other words, it wasn't an especially flattering term.

Sometime between 1512 and 1520, she was kidnapped by Crimean Tatar slavers. At some point, she was taken to Constantinople (Istanbul), where she attracted the attention of Hafsa Sultan, mother of Suleiman, son of Sultan Selim I. When Selim died in 1520, Suleiman became the Ottoman Sultan, with all the power and privilege that came with the title. And one of those privileges was having an extensive harem, of which the young Roxelana was now a part.

It's possible that Roxelana, having no escape from her fate, saw a way for advancement through her own efforts. Soon after Suleiman ascended to the imperial throne, she became known as the Haseki Sultan, or the "favorite concubine," and began not only spending time with him, but advising him as well. Shocking the nobility, he married her in 1533, which was a break with tradition. As sultan, he was expected to marry a free-born foreign woman, preferably one of high rank. To marry a former slave (as Justinian had with Theodora) was unthinkable. On top of that outrage, Roxelana advised him on matters of state, wrote diplomatic letters on his behalf, and consulted on important affairs. These actions aroused considerable jealousy and anger in the harem and the court, especially from her chief rival, a woman named Mahidevran, who had been the sultan's previous favorite.

But it mattered not. Suleiman had determined that Roxelana would bear his heir, a son they named Selim (the future Sultan Selim II). They had six children together, which was another breach of tradition; having more than one son might encourage rivalries between brothers for the throne. Roxelana would continue to wield power and influence throughout her life. Her actions inaugurated an era that came to be known as the "Reign of Women" (1520–1683), a period when Ottoman imperial women exercised considerable power over policies and foreign affairs, even ruling as queen regents.

Roxelana died in 1558 and was buried in a mausoleum at the Süleymaniye Mosque, having gone from a humble priest's daughter to a slave, and then from a royal favorite to quite possibly the most powerful woman in the world at the time.

QUEEN ELIZABETH I'S
LOVE OF SUGAR AND
GINGERBREAD MEN

Queen Elizabeth I (1533–1603) is rightly seen as one of the greatest rulers in English history, a woman who ruled on her own during a time when women were seen as not much more than accessories to men. She was no doubt a match for the men around her; she took no sh*t from them and held her own, despite many attempts to marry her off, assassinate her, and control her. Her reign of nearly forty-five years (1558–1603) is rightly known as the "Elizabethan Age" and is brightened by exceptional works of art, music, and most of all, literature. William Shakespeare, of course, began his career under her rule, and many others followed.

Elizabeth was in every way the model of the courtier and ruler that the Renaissance era demanded. She wrote and spoke several languages, had a good head for military strategy, tried to negotiate the mess of religious problems in England at the time (the conflict between Catholics and Protestants), was a skilled dancer, and was a gifted writer in her own right. She was fond of music, food, and above all, sweets.

Elizabeth loved sugar. Just loved it. At the time, sugar was not something that one could just go down to the market and buy easily; cane sugar was rare, imported, and expensive. The majority of people had to settle for honey and fruit if they wanted to satisfy their sweet cravings, but nobles and royals could indulge as much as they liked. And they did. They put sugar in their wine, they put it on their food, in their cakes, and anywhere else you can think of. Elizabeth also loved gingerbread, and it's believed that she was the one who came up with the idea of making gingerbread figures. These often looked like her courtiers, and she would give these sweets to them as gifts.

And because dental hygiene was not really a thing, you can imagine what began to happen. Elizabeth ate so much sugar that it blackened and rotted her teeth. But she was not put off. In fact, this became something of a fashion statement. Noble women in the court started to blacken their teeth artificially. Why would they do this? Because they were following the "look" of the queen, but more importantly, it gave the impression that they too had eaten a lot of sugar, which sent the message that they were wealthy enough to afford it! Yes, silly fashion trends have been around for a long time, and people have been trying to impress their friends (and people they don't know or even like) long before social media appeared!

PETER THE GREAT:
SINKING HIS TEETH INTO IT

Speaking of teeth, Pyotr Alekseyevich, later known as Peter the Great (1672–1725), ruled Russia from 1682 (yes, at ten years old, though with his brother Ivan until 1696) to his death, and modernized it in ways that would have been almost unthinkable in the generation before him. He expanded Russian power and pushed back against Sweden's domination of the entire Baltic Sea region. He made Russia into a force to be reckoned with and introduced new ideas that were circulating in the European Enlightenment, all to help put Russia on par culturally and intellectually with its western neighbors. He succeeded in replacing several outdated and medieval social and political practices with new ones that were more forward-looking.

He even took on the title of "emperor" as opposed to the old title of "tsar," thinking that it seemed more modern and in keeping with the times, though given that other countries would soon start rebelling against their monarchs altogether, this probably wasn't as much of a reform as he thought it was! He also founded the city of St. Petersburg, which he humbly named after himself; it would be Russia's capitol until the Bolshevik Revolution.

There's no doubt that Peter played an essential part in dragging Russia (kicking and screaming, maybe?) into a more modern world. But Peter had another interest that is little remembered today: he was fascinated by dentistry. What?

He didn't have any official training, of course, but he was said to have witnessed a dentist at work pulling a tooth, and thereafter, he was keenly interested in the dental health of his people. He would offer to pull teeth for his courtiers, who were not happy with the idea, as you can imagine! Some agreed, fearing his anger if they refused. Peter apparently carried a bag of pulled teeth with him to show that he was competent to do the job! One courtier came to Peter and told him that his wife suffered from a terrible toothache, and would he remove the tooth? Peter was only too happy to oblige, only to learn later that there was nothing wrong with the tooth at all, and that her jerk husband had been fighting with her and wanted to get back at her. Peter still seemed pleased with his work.

Peter also had a great interest in anatomy, and—you guessed it—was eager to try conducting autopsies and even simple operations. Again, who was going to say no to him? His autopsies were messy and at least one operation he performed resulted in the death of the patient, though an inquest naturally found that he had nothing to do with it.

Peter might have done a lot to improve Russia's standing in the world and to bring it out from being stuck in the past, but when it came to dentistry and surgery, his methods were positively primitive!

GEORGE WASHINGTON'S
TEETH AND BOOZE

Continuing with our dental theme, you've probably heard the old story that George Washington (1732–99) had wooden teeth. It's an old tale, comparable to his chopping down the cherry tree as a boy and then telling the truth about it. But like that myth, the wooden teeth story is false. He did have teeth that weren't his, but they were someone else's! That's right; some of Washington's false teeth were actually human teeth.

Now, there were various kinds of false teeth in the eighteenth century. Ivory was a common substance used in making them, but it also tended to stain pretty easily, which might be the origin of the idea that his teeth were wooden. Imagine him smiling and seeing a row of dirty tans instead of pearly whites! Brass and even gold were also sometimes found in people's mouths, if they could afford them. But there was a more unsettling source of false teeth, which was teeth from other people, often slaves.

There are records showing that Washington bought teeth from slaves. The poorest in society had been selling teeth for centuries, so it comes as no surprise that there were dentists of his time willing to extract them. It seems in this case that Washington paid them for their teeth; one account shows that he paid a group of slaves 122 shillings in total for nine teeth, which we assume a doctor then implanted in his mouth. Scholars have pointed out that we can't absolutely prove that the teeth were for Washington, but given how bad his own teeth were, it seems likely. The big issue, of course, is whether these slaves had any say in giving

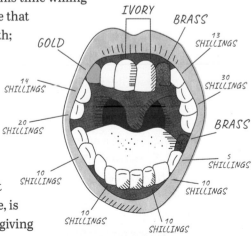

up their teeth. Maybe, maybe not. It does seem that Washington was bothered about the whole practice. He also kept some of his own pulled teeth for later use as dentures.

Whatever his dental hygiene problems, he was also fond of drink in moderation, and after he left office, one of his pet projects was a whiskey distillery. James Anderson, his Scottish farm manager, convinced him in 1797 to open a distillery, convinced that they could make a good profit, and they did. In 1799 alone, the distillery produced 11,000 gallons of the stuff, more than enough to make anyone forget about their teeth problems! The whiskey was not bottled and aged as it is today; it was shipped to taverns in barrels for quick consumption. But Washington died in December of that same year and production soon ceased. The building fell into ruin and burned down in 1814. The distillery was recreated in 2007 and is now open to the public, selling a variety of spirits that could probably make anyone forget about their dental issues.

MARIE ANTOINETTE'S
RUSTIC RETREAT

Poor Marie Antoinette (1755–93) is best known for being Queen of France during the decidedly bloody French Revolution. She and her husband, King Louis XVI, both found themselves on the wrong side of a guillotine blade in 1793, as the revolutionaries decided they'd had enough of aristocrats and monarchs telling them what to do. Of course, only eleven years later, Napoleon would declare himself Emperor of France, which kind of defeated the whole purpose of the revolution. In any case, Marie is often quoted as saying "Let them eat cake," in response to hearing about how the poor didn't have enough bread. Only, she very probably never said this. The image of her being so out of touch with the sufferings of everyday French people is partly true and partly exaggerated.

But one thing she did have was an escape from the luxurious and over-the-top walls of the Palace of Versailles. It was a specially designed village called Hameau de la Reine ("The Queen's Hamlet"). Built in 1783, it offered the young queen a place to get away from the suffocating and rigid constraints of the main palace. It featured an artificial lake, more "rustic" looking buildings (based on designs from Normandy and Flanders), a working farm (with pigs, sheep, and hens), orchards, vineyards, fields, a dairy, a decorative watermill, and more. Produce from the estate was served at royal dinners in the palace. It might seem like the perfect antidote to the gaudy excesses of Versailles. Over the centuries, Marie and her friends have gotten the reputation that they would come down to this little peaceful village to dress in simple clothing and pretend to be farmers, basically cosplaying peasants.

But in fact, inside the plain exteriors, the houses were decorated lavishly, and Marie liked to entertain her friends in small groups, and in the manner to which they were accustomed. She enjoyed walking about the small estate, and had the farm built as an educational tool for her children. It seems she wanted them to have a better idea of where their food actually came from, which is a kind and educational gesture. But since it was not open to the public (of course), many people began to see it as just a private playground for a queen who was so disconnected from her subjects that she enjoyed playing at being poor without understanding their suffering. And it furthered the stereotype that she was a bit of an air-headed little girl, a misconception that would continue all the way into the revolution.

The estate fell into ruin after the execution of the French aristocracy, though Napoleon had the site restored. It's had several restorations since then, and is now open to the public to come and enjoy. It's quite a bit of a trek from the main palace, though!

NAPOLEON, ROMANCE NOVELIST, WAS ONCE ATTACKED BY A FLUFFLE OF RABBITS

Now *there* is a sentence you never thought you would read! And yes, a group of rabbits can be called a herd, a colony, or a fluffle; fluffle is obviously the best choice.

So, what happened? Well, it turns out that once, in July of 1807, Napoleon (1769–1821) decided to have a relaxing day out hunting rabbits. He'd just signed the Treaties of Tilsit, which had ended the war between the French and the Russians, and he wanted to blow off a bit of steam. He asked his chief of staff, Alexandre Berthier, to arrange the hunt.

Berthier put together a lunch, invited some top military commanders, and went to work collecting the rabbits. It's said that he gathered at least several hundred, though some estimates claim the number was as high as 3,000! In any case, a whole lot of rabbits were brought in and held in cages at the edge of a big field. Napoleon set out on his hunt, accompanied by others, and the rabbits were released. He assumed that they would run in all directions; some would flee, but others would scurry about in the field.

Only, that's not what happened. The furious fluffle seemed to gather into a mob and rush toward him as one. The men's amusement turned to concern very quickly, as the bunny brigade got ever closer. They rushed Napoleon, and some of them began charging up his trousers to his coat. The poor emperor tried to shoo them off with his riding crop, and others tried to push back the bunnies with sticks, but it didn't work. Even cracking bullwhips in the air didn't scare them away.

Napoleon had to do something that as a military general, he probably hated: make a hasty retreat. But the bounding bunnies followed him, and even after he ran back to his carriage, they swarmed around him on both sides, some even climbing into the carriage itself as he sped away. The mightiest leader in Europe was defeated by a humble horde of rabbits.

So, what had happened? Were they angry, feral creatures, determined to take revenge for him daring to hunt them? Actually, Berthier had made a mistake and bought tame rabbits from local farmers, rather than trapping wild ones. It seems that these bunnies assumed it was feeding time, and rushed Napoleon and his men because they thought they were getting treats! It was Napoleon's second greatest defeat.

Oh, and yes, in 1795, at the age of twenty-six, Napoleon wrote a short romance novel, *Clisson et Eugénie*, about a soldier and the woman he loves. It wasn't published until after his death, but it survives now in fragments, and is available to buy, if you must read it.

ABRAHAM LINCOLN
WAS A CHAMPION WRESTLER

Honest Abe (1809–65) was the sixteenth president of the United States, famous for leading the Union during the American Civil War, issuing the Emancipation Proclamation, and for his tragic assassination at the hands of John Wilkes Booth. But most people don't know that Lincoln had a celebrated history as a wrestler, and was almost undefeated for twelve years.

Back in the day, it was common for towns to have a wrestling champion whom others would seek out and challenge. Lincoln lived in New Salem, Illinois, and because he was tall (6'4") and weighed a reasonable amount, he took an interest in the sport. He got good at it, and Denton Offutt, the owner of the shop where he worked, started to advertise Lincoln's abilities in order to attract more customers. It worked and his reputation grew, so much so that he was challenged by the local champion, Jack Armstrong. Lincoln eagerly agreed to the match, and sure enough, he won, even though Armstrong was trying to cheat. Armstrong's supporters moved in to attack Lincoln, but Armstrong called them off. He'd gained a new respect for the young man and the two ended up becoming friends.

Lincoln's wrestling reputation only grew from there, and he eventually won the Sangamon County wrestling championship. Over the next twelve years, he would lose only one match out of almost 300! He was known to get pretty psyched up during matches and in victory. After one match, a wound-up Lincoln shouted at the crowd: "I'm the big buck of this lick. If any of you want to try it, come on and whet your horns!" It was basically a "come at me, bro!" for the time. No one did.

His success in politics was at least in part due to his reputation as a wrestling champion. It could only enhance his career prospects, showing him to be a winner and a strong leader. In fact, once when he was giving a General Assembly election speech, a man in the crowd started causing trouble with one of his friends. Lincoln wasn't having any of it, and left the stage, strode up to the man, took hold of him, and threw him twelve feet! After that, he went back to his podium and continued his speech. Imagine that happening in an election these days! Actually, things might end up going that way eventually...

Lincoln's prowess as a wrestler was enough for him to finally be inducted into the National Wrestling Hall of Fame in 1992, another honor to add to his long list of accomplishments.

QUEEN VICTORIA:
LESSER-KNOWN FACTS

Victoria (1819–1901) ruled, rightly or wrongly, over an age when Britain expanded into a world empire, controlling something like one-fourth of the world by the late nineteenth century. She gave her name to the era, and the very word "Victorian" conjures up everything from Charles Dickens novels to the Industrial Revolution, from colonialism to the murky streets of fog-shrouded London. Victoria herself was an improbable queen, ascending to the throne in 1837 only after all of the other eligible heirs had died off. But in time, she proved herself up to the task, and there are a number of interesting but little-known facts about her. Here is a sample:

- You might assume that she was popular with the British people, and generally, she was, though she survived multiple assassination attempts over the course of her life. Several were attempts to shoot her, while one involved a man who managed to get close enough to hit her on the head with his cane! She suffered only a bruise. Several of these would-be assassins were found not guilty by reason of insanity and sentenced to asylums, while one was banished. Each time she survived one of these potential murders, her popularity grew. Her security came up with the idea of an armored parasol (lined with chain mail, to be exact) as a way of protecting her!

· Height was definitely not her strong point. Despite her sometimes imposing presence, she barely stood five feet tall.

· After having nine children in seventeen years, she had some pointed views about them and childbirth in general. After her first child, she remarked: "It seems like a dream having a child." But when one of her daughters gave birth, she said, "I think much more of our being like a cow or a dog at such moments." As for her opinion about women's fates: "When I think of a merry, happy, and free young girl—and look at the ailing aching state a young wife is generally doomed to—which you can't deny is the penalty of marriage."

· Possibly related to the above entry, she was known to spy on her children, hiring various experts to keep an eye on them and report back to her.

· She also wished for her youngest daughter, Beatrice, not to marry, and to remain by her side as a companion. When Beatrice went ahead and got married anyway, Victoria didn't speak to her for six months.

· While she dearly loved her husband, Prince Albert, they could get into some amazing fights. Her temper was so much that Albert would sometimes resort to slipping notes under her door, so as to avoid talking to her in person!

· On the happier side, Victoria and Albert loved Christmas, and it was that love that introduced Britain to the concept of the Christmas tree (until then mostly a German tradition), beginning in 1848. When an image of the royal family decorating a tree was published, it became a sensation, and Brits wanted to imitate them. So they did, and a new British holiday tradition was born!

TEDDY ROOSEVELT
BRUSHES OFF AN ASSASSINATION ATTEMPT

Roosevelt (1858–1919) was a larger-than-life character, president of the United States between 1901 and 1909. He was opinionated, controversial, and famed for his motto, "Speak softly and carry a big stick," when it came to foreign policy. But he felt that two terms was enough, and left office in March of 1909. However, duty called when a schism developed in the Republican Party between its conservatives and its progressives. Roosevelt decided to create a new Progressive Party (the "Bull Moose" party) and run for office again. But he'd definitely made enemies.

On October 14, 1912, he was in Milwaukee to give a campaign speech. A disturbed man named John Flammang Schrank believed that the ghost of assassinated President William McKinley (Roosevelt had been his Vice President) was telling him to kill Roosevelt. Outside of the Gilpatrick Hotel, Schrank managed to get within ten feet of Roosevelt and opened fire, shooting him with a .32 caliber bullet. Schrank was subdued and might have been lynched on the spot, but Roosevelt called for him to be spared and taken in.

Roosevelt should have died, but by good fortune, he had an eyeglasses case in his coat pocket, which was also stuffed with a copy of a speech that he was about to give. These items slowed the bullet and he basically only suffered a flesh wound. Roosevelt had anatomical knowledge and was an experienced hunter, so he was able to conclude that the bullet had not pierced his lung. Therefore, he declined immediate medical attention and went ahead with giving his speech!

He took the speech papers out of his coat pocket, and they had blood on them. He allegedly said, "Ladies and gentlemen, I don't know whether you fully understand that I have just been shot. You see, it takes more than one bullet to kill a Bull Moose." This is a great quote, but its validity is somewhat in doubt. But what isn't in doubt is that his speech took over an hour. Only then did he go to a hospital for treatment.

An X-ray showed that the bullet had stopped in his chest muscle. The doctors who examined him decided that it was better to just leave it there, rather than risk complications by removing it surgically. The bullet remained inside of him for the rest of his life.

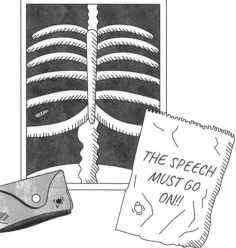

His presidential opponents, Howard Taft and Woodrow Wilson, suspended their campaigns until Teddy was well enough to start campaigning again, which was only two weeks later. He was asked if the incident would affect him or his campaign, and he told the reporter: "I'm fit as a Bull Moose."

You might think that this incident would have rallied the public around him, but he went on to lose the election to Wilson in a 42% to 27% vote split, while Taft got 23%. So much for toughness.

QUEEN ELIZABETH II
HAD AN UNUSUAL
WARTIME OCCUPATION

By the time of her death on September 8, 2022, Queen Elizabeth II had been Britain's longest-reigning monarch, being queen for a staggering seventy years. She was without a doubt one of the most famous people in the world, and the best-known monarch of any nation, anywhere. She witnessed Britain go from a fading colonial power to exiting from the European Union, and many considered her a symbol of the nation through good times and bad.

There is something endearing and yet oddly untouchable about Britain's royal family. People seem to both love and hate them; they love reading about them and their troubles in the tabloids, but will cheer for them when they make public appearances. The queen herself had very high approval ratings, regardless of what her relatives did!

So it might seem a bit odd that this essence of Britishness, this model of upper-class civility spent time during the last months of World War II engaged in a rather mundane, but very important job: she was an auto mechanic. She had already been given an honorary title, Colonel of the Grenadier Guards, and when she turned eighteen in 1944, she joined the Auxiliary Territorial Service (the ATS), the women's branch of the British Army that unmarried women under the age of thirty were expected to join. She was given no special treatment and joined up as any other young woman would; her father, the king, had specifically requested this. Elizabeth remains the only female member of the royal family to have ever served in the British Army.

In March of 1945, she began training as a mechanic, learning both truck and ambulance driving and maintenance. She qualified the next month, and newspapers were quick to name her "Princess Auto Mechanic." She could have chosen from a good number of professions open to women, including operating a searchlight, ammunition inspector, and even joining an anti-aircraft unit. But as the war was winding down, she became proficient enough in vehicle repair that she could change tires and take apart and reassemble engines. Her designation was truck mechanic No. 230873. According to her and her friends, she enjoyed getting her hands dirty and getting lost in the work.

After the war, she went back to her "royal" duties, but one likes to think that, if a royal family automobile ever broke down somewhere, she could have hopped out and had it up and running again in no time!

FIDEL CASTRO
AND HIS SPORTY EARLY DAYS

Castro (1926–2016) was, of course, infamous as the communist leader (many would say dictator) of Cuba, whose overthrowing of the US-backed Cuban military dictatorship in 1958 caused so much American panic and led to a near war during the Cuban Missile Crisis of 1962. Castro defied the American juggernaut next door and stayed in power for decades, retiring in 2008 and finally dying in 2016. This was despite being isolated from the United States, there being an embargo on Cuban goods (Cuban cigars still found their way into the homes of wealthy American connoisseurs, however), and Americans being forbidden from vacationing on the island (though they would often go to Mexico and then sneak over to Cuba, anyway).

Castro was a hardline communist who embraced the Soviet Union and caused unending headaches for American presidents, while some Latin American nations hailed him as a hero for standing up to the superpower 93 miles north across the Straits of Florida. But he had an interesting prior life that not many people know about: he had a passionate love for baseball.

There are multiple versions of his early life and flirtations with the game. One says that he was a star pitcher at the University of Havana in the later 1940s, and attracted the interest of some Major League Baseball scouts. Some of these thought he had talent, while others didn't. But a few teams sent some of their hitters down to test him out, and he was eventually offered tryouts with teams like the Pittsburgh Pirates and even the New York Yankees. But he failed to impress and was sent away, which led to his growing anti-American sentiments.

However, another story says that he was offered a contract with the New York Giants (before they moved to San Francisco, of course), but he turned it down to study law, instead. The mind boggles at what might have happened in world events if Castro had gone to the Giants and had a career in baseball rather than in politics. How different would the world have been?

There's a wonderful excitement in this urban legend that gives us one of those tantalizing "what if" scenarios. The problem is, there's almost no evidence that these stories are true, even though they get bandied about on the internet all the time. Castro definitely loved baseball, played in college, and would go out to pitch in exhibition games in Havana from time to time. In the early days of his rule, the MLB even sent some teams down to Cuba for

FIDEL
CASTRO

games. But there's no evidence that he played professionally, much less tried out for any MLB teams. If he ever did, the record of it is lost now.

So, he probably never intended to try to be a professional baseball player in the United States, but his enthusiasm for the sport was remarkable, considering how much he tended to rail against the United States and all that it stood for. A lot of people would consider baseball to be one of the most "American" pastimes there is, and yet here was a communist revolutionary eagerly embracing the sport his whole life.

KIM JONG-IL'S
OBSESSION WITH MOVIES
LED TO KIDNAPPING

The family of dictators who have ruled North Korea since 1948 has never been known for being what we might call predictable, or even stable. Kim Jong-Il, who ruled the infamously reclusive nation from 1994 to 2011, had an interesting hobby: he loved movies. So much so that he had a problem with the North Korean film "industry." He said, "When I watch our films... they are all dogmatic. Why do our films always have the same ideological stories? Why are there so many crying scenes? This isn't a funeral... We don't have any films that get into film festivals?"

Well, it might have something to do with being the most reclusive and paranoid nation on Earth, but who knows? And all that crying—well, yeah, what else is there to do in North Korea? In any case, Kim was more familiar with the films of the South Koreans and other countries, and he wanted North Korean films to have more pizzazz, more creativity. So what did he do? The most logical thing he could think of: he kidnapped a top director and actress from South Korea and had them brought to the North, where he basically begged them to make some decent films!

In 1978, Kim had director Shin Sang-ok and his wife Choi Eun-hee kidnapped and smuggled into North Korea. Choi was tricked into coming after receiving a fake offer for a business opportunity in Hong Kong. When she went to meet with the alleged businessmen, she was kidnapped by North Korean agents and taken. Kim even greeted her and thanked her for coming! Shin traveled to the North a few months after Choi, but it's not clear if he was also kidnapped or went willingly.

In any case, Kim kept them separate from each other, and neither knew about the other being in North Korea. He told each of them that the North Korean film industry was "useless" and that they could show the nation an example of how to make a decent film. The whole thing was bizarre on many levels: not only the appalling act of the abduction itself, but Kim's acknowledgement that the country's so-called utopia was basically a disaster, and that the propaganda films were no longer working. Of course, Kim put his own spin on it, in that North Korea was failing because people were too happy and content, and they needed to be "whipped onwards" to improve!

It turned out that Kim was a great fan of the work of both Choi and Shin, since he was probably the only person in the North who'd watched their films. He was the head of the nation's Propaganda and Agitation Department (great name!), and fancied himself to be quite the cinephile. In 1983, he "invited" them to his birthday party, and they were shocked to realize that both were in the same captive situation. Over the next two years, they made seventeen films together for Kim, working almost constantly; it's not like they had a choice. Amazingly, Choi and Shin were given the freedom to do what they wanted creatively, a drastic change from the tightly-controlled state propaganda content of other North Korean films.

The two traveled to various foreign film festivals under the watchful eye of agents, but in Vienna in 1986, they managed to escape and obtain asylum at the US Embassy. They lived in the United States until 1999, before returning to South Korea. Kim was outraged and set about erasing evidence of their time in North Korea, acting as if they were honored guests who'd betrayed him. The whole story is just another in an endless collection of tales about this strange, reclusive, abusive nation.

JIMMY CARTER'S
UFO

Jimmy Carter was a one-term president (1977–80), whose presidency coincided with several earth-shattering events, including the People's Temple mass suicides in Guyana and the Iranian hostage crisis, following the revolution there in 1979. But back before he was even governor of Georgia, he had another encounter, one that he was never able to fully explain. In October of 1969, along with ten to twelve other witnesses, Carter saw the "darnedest thing": a UFO in the night sky. In a 2005 interview with *GQ* magazine, Carter reiterated what he and several others saw in the early evening:

"All of a sudden, one of the men looked up and said, 'Look, over in the west!' And there was a bright light in the sky. We all saw it. And then the light, it got closer and closer to us. And then it stopped, I don't know how far away, but it stopped beyond the pine trees. And all of a sudden it changed color to blue, and then it changed to red, then back to white. And we were trying to figure out what in the world it could be, and then it receded into the distance."

He also noted that it was "about the size of the moon." He never stated that he believed that it was an alien spacecraft; he said only that it was unidentified, and he vowed that he would never ridicule or look down on others

who had seen strange things in the night sky. Various skeptics have said that what he probably saw was an Air Force project to study the atmosphere using chemical clouds, which at certain times of day (dusk and dawn) would glow in some of the same colors that Carter reported.

In any case, during the presidential campaign in 1976, Carter vowed to look deeper into the UFO phenomenon and reveal any information he could that might be withheld from the American public and scientists. But after his election, he backed off from this pledge, citing concerns about national security and defense. Other presidents, including Bill Clinton and Barack Obama, made similar promises during their campaigns, only to go back on them after taking office, as well. Make of that what you will... is the truth out there?

MIKHAIL GORBACHEV,
GRAMMY WINNER

There is no doubt that Gorbachev (1931–2022) changed the world. Many remember him as the Soviet leader who introduced the concept of glasnost, or "openness," to the Soviet Union in the 1980s, and who realized that the Eastern Block of nations was something that the Soviets could no longer afford to keep propping up against Western Europe and the United States. He was an advocate for Perestroika, a reform movement that sought to modernize the Soviet Union after decades of stagnation.

Loyalists viewed him as a traitor and tried to overthrow him in a coup, which failed. He returned to power, but the Soviet Union broke up in 1991, leaving the United States as the world's only "superpower." Some historians and activists have pointed out that the world's love affair with him is likely misplaced, since he engaged in many of the same oppressive behaviors as previous Soviet leaders had.

Still, for his efforts in cooling off the Cold War and releasing communist Eastern European nations to be free (many of which are now members of the European Union) he was awarded a Nobel Peace Prize in 1990, though he admitted to having mixed feelings about it, and many Soviets saw it as nothing more than a symbol of anti-Soviet propaganda.

But what many people don't know is that he also won a Grammy in February, 2004. No, it wasn't for singing on an album of Russian folk songs (though that would have been remarkable!), but rather for contributing narration to a new version of Prokofiev's *Peter and the Wolf*, along with Bill Clinton and actress Sophia Lauren. The recording was created to honor the fiftieth anniversary of the death of Prokofiev, and was a big affair, with new music and new texts commissioned. Gorbachev arranged for his share of any profits from the recording to be donated to the Green Cross International, an environmental organization that he founded in 1993.

It might seem that a recording featuring Gorbachev and Clinton was a sure thing for at least one major award, but winning a Grammy does make for an unusual achievement for the communist world leader that *Time* magazine proclaimed as its "Man of the Decade" in the 1980s.

SAPARMURAT NIYAZOV:
NOT THE AVERAGE
STRONGMAN

Niyazov (1940–2006) is the most flamboyant, outrageous, egotistical, and colorful dictator you've probably never heard of. He was declared president for life of the Central Asian nation of Turkmenistan from 1990 until he died in 2006. At first a loyalist to the Soviet Union, he was quite happy to continue keeping the nation under his thumb after the Soviet break-up.

Niyazov had a high opinion of himself, to say the least, and set about creating a cult of personality to rival that of the Kims in North Korea. He wrote an autobiography, the *Ruhnama*, that was, of course, the greatest story ever told. He required that it be read in all schools, universities, and government offices, and that it be kept in all mosques. Those looking to work for the government were tested in their knowledge of the book, as was anyone who wanted a driver's license (?!). He had a statue of the book constructed to be displayed in the capitol, and then awarded himself a literary prize.

He renamed towns, the airport, schools and universities, and pretty much anything else you can think of after himself. Not content with that, he renamed the days of the week and months of the year after important figures in Turkmen history... and after himself, of course. He created and imposed a new alphabet (because why not?), based on the Latin one instead of Cyrillic. He even renamed bread after his mother! He saw to it that his portraits hung everywhere, and reworked the national anthem to give himself credit for being so awesome; people were forced to listen to it constantly. But they couldn't listen to a lot of other music. He banned opera and ballet, recorded music, and even lip-syncing, as well as internet access.

Smoking? Forget it. Men with long hair? Forbidden. The circus? Who needs it? No dogs in the capitol? That was a law. Free press? Ha ha. Women couldn't wear makeup on TV, and he even prohibited gold teeth, saying that if you wanted strong teeth, you should just chew on bones! More wisdom from this obviously amazing leader.

The year before he died, he closed all hospitals and libraries in the country except for those in the capitol, Ashgabat, stating that if people were ill, they could just come to the city. Also, doctors no longer swore the Hippocratic Oath, but an oath to him, instead. Not surprisingly, Turkmenistan was ranked as having the lowest life expectancy in all of Central Asia. He also ordered that the last two years of people's pensions be paid back, while he kept something like $3 billion in his own accounts outside the nation.

As you can imagine, he was pretty nuts, an extreme narcissist, and a self-styled cult leader. And no, he wasn't all that popular. After he died, the next president, Deputy Prime Minister Gurbanguly Berdimuhamedow (a dentist, by the way... what's with all the teeth in this section?), started undoing much of Niyazov's nonsense, though there is still one golden statue to him. Berdimuhamedow, however, seemed quite happy to keep some of the dictatorial policies in place and the nation is by no means a "free" one, even now.

ANGELA MERKEL'S
REMARKABLE BACKGROUND

Merkel was Chancellor of Germany from 2005 to 2021, and the nation's first woman in that position. Her role and importance was such that she was often seen as the *de facto* leader of the European Union (Germany and France have always been the EU's two powerhouses), and at times even as the coveted "leader of the free world," as turmoil engulfed both Britain and the United States from 2016 onward. Usually seen as a very capable and strong leader, Merkel handled any number of crises and issues in her time, up to and including the COVID pandemic.

Indeed, some said that she was especially well-equipped to deal with a major health issue like COVID because of her unique scientific background. Though she'd made a life as a career politician, Merkel's education and early work were in the sciences.

Though born in what was at the time West Germany, she grew up in communist East Germany, and studied physics in the 1970s. She later attended and worked for the Central Institute for Physical Chemistry at the Academy of Sciences in Berlin-Adlershof between 1978 and 1990. She earned her Ph.D. in 1986, writing a doctoral thesis on Quantum Chemistry, which is the application of quantum mechanics to chemical systems. As you do.

She continued to work for the Academy, and published several papers, including "Theoretical approach to reactions of polyatomic molecules," and "Chimaerism and erythroid marker expression after microinjection of human acute myeloid leukaemia cells into murine blastocysts." Wow!

But she was still stuck in East Germany, and after being approached by the Ministry for State Security (the Stasi) to become an informant for them, she refused. When the Berlin Wall fell and Eastern Europe freed itself from the grips of the crumbling Soviet Union, Merkel decided to jump ship from a potentially lucrative science career and take up the much more uncertain work of politics. She joined the new *Demokratischer Aufbruch* ("Democratic Beginning") party, and Leader Wolfgang Schnur appointed her as its press spokeswoman in February, 1990. But it was soon revealed that Schnur had been a member of the hated Stasi, so he was expelled (he'd probably been trying to hitch a ride to the new movement to save himself). This revelation damaged the DA, which only picked up four seats in the election. But because it was a member party of the new Alliance for Germany, which won the election by a landslide, Merkel's political aspirations continued and she didn't have to return to scientific research.

Her political career really took off in the 1990s, and by the 2000s, she was in a position to make a real mark, first as leader of the opposition from 2002 to 2005, and finally as Chancellor from 2005 to 2021. Throughout her time as leader, she maintained an interest in scientific topics, such as Artificial Intelligence, quantum computing, and clean energy. She regularly held meetings with scientists and stressed the importance of research and development in securing and improving Germany's future.

Her combination of skills from very different backgrounds made her one of the most influential and unique world leaders in modern times.

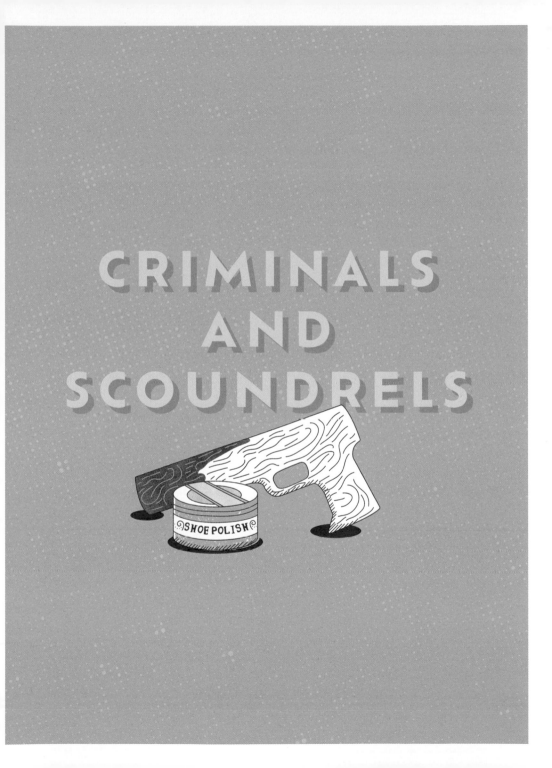

CRIMINALS
AND
SCOUNDRELS

THE REAL
DRACULA

Bram Stoker's late nineteenth-century classic has thrilled generations of readers and inspired countless other vampire tales, from *Buffy* to *Twilight*. But while vampire legends are almost inseparable from Eastern Europe, the inspiration for the blood-drinking count was no vampire. He was a prince, Vlad Dracula ("Son of the Dragon," 1431–76), who ruled the small nation of Wallachia, in what is now southern Romania, at various times during the fifteenth century.

Throughout those years, the Ottoman Turks were pressing ever further into Europe and trying to take the ancient Byzantine city of Constantinople, which they finally succeeded in doing in 1453, to the horror of Christian Europe. This defeat spurred many rulers to resist the Turkish onslaught, none more so that the Prince of Wallachia, who was said to be ready to do whatever it took to keep the invaders out of his land.

A German poet and musician named Michel Beheim heard rumors about this tyrant from a monk who had allegedly escaped his terror. Vlad Dracula, also known as *Țepeș*, or "the Impaler," was terrorizing his own people in his efforts to resist the Ottomans. In 1463, Beheim wrote the *Story of a Bloodthirsty Madman Called Dracula of Wallachia*, wherein he recounted all of Dracula's horrific deeds. The poem was performed for the Holy Roman Emperor and was an immediate hit, a kind of late-medieval horror story.

Vlad Dracula ruled Wallachia with an iron fist, eager to root out traitors, collaborators, and those he saw as suffering from moral laxity. His most famous punishment was to impale victims on wooden stakes, an agonizing execution that could take days to kill the victim. He would leave the bodies on display as a public warning, and soon the whole country dwelled in his fearful shadow. It's possible that tens of thousands of people died in this horrific way, whether criminals or innocent victims. Vlad delighted in other tortures and displays of brutality as well. It was said that he had victims

flayed alive, that he forced some to eat the bodies of others before they too were killed, boiled others alive, and once even ordered that ambassadors to his court have their caps nailed to their heads, for failing to take them off in deference to him.

His most notorious crime was his "forest of the impaled," his terror tactic to turn back the Turks. Knowing that his army was not large enough to fight the Ottomans in the field, he captured as many Turkish soldiers and others as he could, and then set about drawing the Ottoman army toward his desired location, an open field where he had impaled these Turkish forces. There were thousands of them on stakes as far as the eye could see, a true "forest." The sultan was so overwhelmed by this that he turned around and left the country, saying he could not fight such a man who was capable of doing something so terrible. It was a psychological terror tactic that worked and saved Wallachia from invasion. But Dracula was soon deposed and held prisoner in Hungary from 1462. He came back to briefly rule Wallachia again in the 1470s, but was killed in battle. For some in modern Romania, he is still a folk hero.

So, are these appalling stories true? The Holy Roman Emperor had no love for the Hungarians and Wallachians, so it's very possible that Beheim made up some of the most horrible tales about Dracula. But the impalement reports are very likely to be true. Vlad was a brutal ruler willing to do anything to preserve his nation's independence. And for a while, he stopped the Turks in their tracks.

JOHN DILLINGER'S
AMAZING ESCAPE

Dillinger (1903–34) was a notorious American gangster during the Great Depression. He led the so-called Dillinger Gang, which, in a very short time, robbed twenty-four banks and even four police stations! The sheer audacity of his crimes was shocking and made him famous. In fact, he loved the notoriety, and even some media outlets tried to portray him as more of a romantic Robin Hood–kind of guy than a dangerous criminal. The amazing thing is, he'd spent much of the 1920s in prison, and only started his true crime spree after his release on parole in 1933. He vowed, "I will be the meanest bastard you ever saw when I get out of here." He was released at the height of the Depression, and had no options other than a return to a life of crime, which he relished, as proven by his run on banks and police stations!

But by 1934, things had starting really getting out of hand, and he was charged with the killing of a police officer after his gang robbed First Bank of East Chicago on January 15, 1934. He was arrested in Arizona and taken back to Indiana to stand trial. He was incarcerated in the Lake County Jail in Crown Point, Indiana, which the police said was inescapable. Knowing what a threat Dillinger was, they even posted extra guards. They shouldn't have bothered.

On the morning of March 3, 1934, Dillinger escaped from the jail without a shot being fired. So much for "inescapable!" So what happened? There are different reports, but the most popular says that Dillinger managed to carve a fake pistol out of wood and blacked it with shoe polish, one that looked convincing enough that he could bluff his way out. That morning, he had been doing exercises, and as the deputies came by, he pulled out his "pistol" and demanded they let him out. Knowing that Dillinger was dangerous, they didn't want to take any chances. They called for two extra guards, and Dillinger was able to lock them up and escape using their keys; none of them ever checked the gun. Herbert Barr, the deputy sheriff on duty, was asleep the entire time, and apparently didn't wake up until ten minutes after Dillinger was out. Some researchers think that Dillinger was able to have an actual gun smuggled into the jail, but even the FBI at the time listed it as a wooden replica, so who knows? Either way, it was an audacious escape.

Dillinger offered to take another prisoner, Henry Jelemik, with him, but Jelemik refused, telling Dillinger that he was "too hot"; i.e., he was the most wanted man in America, and Jelemik didn't want to be anywhere near him. He preferred jail to freedom at Dillinger's side.

And this was probably a wise choice.

Dillinger went on another crime spree, with the Feds hot on his tail. There were shootouts and narrow escapes, but by July, he was in hiding. He paid for plastic surgery to alter his face, but was given an overdose of ether and nearly suffocated. One evening in July of 1934, he was seen entering the Biograph Theater to watch a movie. The Feds were onto him. After leaving, he was told to surrender and fled to an alley. He might have pulled out his own gun (there are different versions of the story), but the agents were ready and shot him multiple times, killing him. After he was carted away, witnesses were seen dipping their handkerchiefs and newspapers into puddles of his blood on the ground. Apparently, they wanted to take a bit of it away as souvenirs. That's kind of gross, but such was Dillinger's notoriety that a lot of people wanted a connection to him, no matter how small.

AL CAPONE'S CHARITY WORK AND TAX PROBLEMS

Al Capone (1899–1947) is a legendary gangster, famous for his role as the boss of the Chicago Outfit during Prohibition. He was eyeball deep in the world of organized crime and involved in a very lucrative bootlegging operation, while the mayor of Chicago and often the police looked the other way. But for all of his crimes, the one thing they finally got him on was something that everyone fears, or at least finds annoying: taxes.

Capone was hardly secretive about his activities. He would show up at public functions, such as sports matches, and make a number of donations to charities with his ill-gotten money. He funded a soup kitchen that at one point served up to 120,000 (!) meals a day to the hungry, at breakfast, lunch, and dinner. It was an amazing exercise in PR that endeared him to vast numbers of Chicagoans, who (perhaps rightly) saw that he was doing more for them than the mayor or the Illinois government. Some saw him as a "modern-day Robin Hood," though his methods were brutal.

The infamous St. Valentine's Day Massacre of February 14, 1929, is believed to have been orchestrated by his gang (though he was away at the time). Seven members of the "Bugs" Moran mob were gunned down by a rival gang pretending to be police. The Bureau of Investigation (the forerunner of the FBI) became involved when Capone refused to appear before a federal grand jury, even after being subpoenaed. He managed to beat a contempt of court charge by paying a fine. But this was the start of several troubles and arrests for Capone, though either nothing really stuck or he managed to get light sentences for things like weapons possession and other contempt charges.

The feds wanted to take him down and devised a creative way of doing it: tax evasion. They eventually charged him with twenty-two counts. Capone tried to brag that he would strike a deal with the judge, but that fell through. He was convicted on five of the counts in late 1931, and sentenced to eleven years in prison; plus, he was ordered to pay all taxes owed. They couldn't get him on murder, weapons, or bootlegging charges, but tax evasion did the trick.

He ended up serving a portion of his time at Alcatraz (beginning in 1934), the prison on the island in San Francisco Bay. He was one of its earliest inmates, but by then, he was already suffering from various health problems, including STDs and cocaine withdrawal. During his time at Alcatraz, he was diagnosed with syphilis dementia, so he was eventually transferred to a low-security prison in Los Angeles. He was released early, in 1939, but his health continued to deteriorate. He returned to his home in Florida to live out a quiet life.

A year before he died, his doctor noted that he had the mental ability of a twelve year old. He had a stroke in January of 1947 and died of a heart attack soon after. The mighty Robin Hood of the Depression era was no more.

JAMES "WHITEY" BULGER
AND MIND CONTROL

Conspiracy theories are all over the internet these days, from fairly mild to completely wild. Most people just roll their eyes and dismiss them out of hand, which might be a good idea. But sometimes, a good conspiracy theory is all too true. Such was the case with the CIA's MK-Ultra program, designed in the 1950s to see if mind control could really work. Yes, this went about as well as you might think. The United States government was concerned that the Soviet Union had come up with ways of brainwashing people. The fear was that they might pull this off with some prisoners and then release them, only to have them commit crimes or espionage once back in America without even knowing they'd done it. So MK-Ultra was created to test just how well someone could be brainwashed (or not) with drugs, sensory deprivation, shocks, and other unpleasant procedures.

Meanwhile, James Joseph "Whitey" Bulger (1929–2018) was something of a legend in Boston's organized crime scene. He was guilty of many crimes, including extortion, drug trafficking, racketeering, and worst of all, murder. And yet, he doesn't seem to have killed anyone until after a very specific series of events in his life: while incarcerated in Atlanta, Bulger was offered the chance to participate in the MK-Ultra program.

He was part of one of the LSD experiments. He was told that the study was to try to find a cure for schizophrenia, and he was convinced to participate as a way of making amends to society, as well as getting some time off his sentence. During the period of testing, he was given at least fifty doses of LSD in high concentrations. He later spoke about how one of the doses affected him: "The room would change shape. Hours of paranoia and feeling violent. We experienced horrible periods of living nightmares and even blood coming out of the walls. Guys turning to skeletons in front of me. I saw a camera change into the head of a dog. I felt like I was going insane."

He was also asked leading questions like, "would you ever murder anyone?" And interestingly, he was not involved in killing until after these experiments. Did the researchers succeed in planting an idea in him, after all? For years afterward, he had nightmares and hallucinations. It's known that LSD can be very beneficial in treating some disorders, but not in the concentrations that Bulger received it. He was paroled in 1965, and then began his rise to the top of the Boston organized crime world, where he gained a reputation for his ruthlessness. He avoided arrest until 2011. In 2013, he was sentenced to life in prison. In 2018, he was beaten to death by some of his fellow inmates, less than twenty-four hours after being transferred to the United States Penitentiary at Hazelton in West Virginia.

Bulger was just one of many participants subjected to MK-Ultra's experiments, pretty much just to see what would happen. Like Bulger, inmates were often told that if they took part in the program, they would have their

sentences reduced or gain other perks. And it wasn't just criminals; soldiers, the mentally ill, and those seen as "deviant" were all subjected to various tests with drugs, electric shocks, and more, to see how they would react and if they could be controlled. Of course, this was outrageously illegal, so much so that the whole project was shut down in 1963, and then a lot of the files were conveniently lost or "accidentally" destroyed before a 1977 commission could investigate them in more detail.

Did MK-Ultra turn Bulger and possibly many others into violent criminals? The jury is still out.

JEAN-BERNARD LASNAUD'S
AMAZINGLY ILLEGAL WEBSITE

Jean-Bernard Lasnaud was arrested in 2002 in Switzerland, on charges of arms dealing and selling illegal goods. He'd been wanted for several years by the Argentinian government and Interpol, as well as by various European courts on charges of fraud and illegal arms trading. Now, you might think that he was on the run, hiding out in some obscure location in a small country, always looking over his shoulder to make sure that the law wasn't closing in on him. Actually, no. He lived for ten years in a gated community near Fort Lauderdale, Florida, quite out in the open, as a local resident. Oh, and he operated a website that sold all kinds of weapons, from missiles to fighter jets, to literally anyone who visited the site and could pay. This was back in the wilder days of the internet, when the law hadn't yet caught up with the tech.

This crazy nose-thumbing is even more astonishing given who some of his clients probably were, and how much product he moved. He publicly boasted that his Caribbean companies sold between $1 million and $2.5 million worth of arms every year (at least). Some of his clients likely included China and Somalia; we say "likely" because their involvement with him has not been definitely proven. He also supplied Argentinian weapons by the thousands of tons to Croatia during the Balkan war, as well as to Ecuador between 1992 and 1995. And he didn't even try to hide it. Former Argentinian President Carlos Menem was involved in the deals; he was convicted, but never served time, and even ran again for office.

If you needed weapons or other arms? You could just go to his website, click what you needed, add it to your cart, whip out your credit card, and you were good to go! Okay, it was a little bit more complex than that, but the website definitely gave prospective buyers the information they needed to purchase all kinds of weaponry.

The big question is, why wasn't Lasnaud arrested earlier? It's not like he was in hiding. Interpol had issued a so-called "red notice" for his arrest in 1999, meaning it was urgent, an international arrest warrant. Yet American authorities seemed content to let him run his highly unusual web-based business from his luxury home in Florida. It was only when some reporters began digging into his activities that the pressure was finally applied. Investigative reporter Julia Reynolds dug into the story and reported on it, which seemed to make Lasnaud nervous. He left the US, and her reporting team alerted Interpol. Lasnaud was picked up in Switzerland, finally ending his outrageous experiment in internet commerce.

SCIENTISTS
AND
INVENTORS

MERIT PTAH OR PESESHET:
WHO WAS THE FIRST
KNOWN FEMALE PHYSICIAN?

The ancient Egyptians kept pretty meticulous records about much of their culture and society over several thousand years, which has given historians and archaeologists amazing opportunities to discover and learn ever more about these fascinating people. But many questions remain, and many more will never be answered. It's the frustrating way of things with ancient history.

One of the more intriguing questions concerns the identity of the first known female doctor. For many decades, that honor has gone to a woman named Merit Ptah ("Beloved of Ptah," the god of sculptors and craftspeople, though interestingly, the goddess Sekhmet was more associated with healing). She was said to have lived during Egypt's Second Dynasty, around the year 2700 BCE, and to have been the royal court physician. Since the 1930s, many have lauded her as the first named female physician, and possibly the first physician in general.

But there is a problem: she didn't exist. The mystery woman behind Merit Ptah was named Peseshet, who lived sometime between the twenty-fifth and twenty-second centuries BCE. The confusion came from the tomb of a man (possibly a high priest), that names his mother, Peseshet, as "Overseer of Healer Women." She also had the titles "King's Acquaintance," and "Overseer of Funerary-Priests of the King's Mother." She might have been involved in the training of midwives.

The confusion seems to have come when medical historian and doctor Kate Campbell Hurd-Mead wrote about Peseshet in the 1930s and conflated/confused her with another hypothetical doctor, Merit Ptah, who allegedly lived earlier. But there are no records that a Merit Ptah who was the court physician ever existed.

Jakub Kwiecinski at the University of Colorado Anschutz Medical Campus explains:

> "Unfortunately, Hurd-Mead in her own book accidentally mixed up the name of the ancient healer, as well as the date when she lived, and the location of the tomb... And so, from a misunderstood case of an authentic Egyptian woman healer, Peseshet, a seemingly earlier Merit Ptah, 'the first woman physician' was born."

Merit Ptah has become a symbol for many feminists, as wells as activists who have tried to get more women involved in STEM and the medical professions in particular, so this might seem like a bit of a blow. But the reality is that a woman named Peseshet really existed and she still proves the importance that women with various duties had in the corridors of power in ancient Egypt.

PYTHAGORAS'
BIZARRE RELATIONSHIP WITH BEANS

Everyone knows something about Pythagoras (c.570–c.495 BCE), the ancient Greek mathematician and philosopher who had a devoted following. His work influenced that of Plato and Aristotle, and for centuries, writers from many cultures and backgrounds attributed all kinds of revolutionary mathematical thinking to him. He has been credited with, among other things, developing the Pythagorean theorem (which everyone remembers from high school geometry!), coming up with Pythagorean tuning for stringed instruments (a system used well into the Middle Ages and beyond), the Theory of Proportions (in geometry and later in art), the fact that the Earth is a sphere, and that the evening star is actually the planet Venus. He might have also been the first to call himself a philosopher, which literally means a "lover of wisdom."

How much he was responsible for any of these things is up for debate. Some more cynical historians think that he probably had nothing to do with any of them! In any case, his biography is a bit mythical. He was a firm believer in the concept of "transmigration of souls," or reincarnation. It's said that he was a vegetarian (at least according to Ovid), but he had one particular and peculiar amendment to that; he apparently avoided fava beans and told his followers never to touch them, much less eat them.

Because they caused gas, he maintained that when said gas, ahem, emitted from someone, it would take away some of one's "breath of life." Even more, he insisted that these beans contained the souls of the dead. "Eating fava beans and gnawing on the heads of one's parents are one and the same," he said (or not). Well, that's an image you won't soon forget!

And did he mean that by eating fava beans, you were absorbing these disembodied souls into your own body? Or that when farting, you would expel the now-beanless soul back into the world? The mind boggles!

His avoidance of these beans led to his own demise. In most of the versions of his death (yes, there are more than one!), he dies because he is running for his life for some reason, but will not tread on a bean field, and so whoever is chasing him catches up with him and kills him (by slitting his throat, burning him alive, or performing some other awful deed). He didn't want to step on and damage any beans and presumably harm the souls within them, so he sacrificed his own life instead. Remember that the next time you're in the grocery store's bean aisle.

TYCHO BRAHE:
HIS FALSE NOSE,
AND HIS DRUNKEN PET

You might never have heard of Tycho Brahe (1546–1601). He was a Danish astronomer who was known for being a bit eccentric, and as a member of the aristocracy, he was outrageously wealthy. At one point, he owned something like 1% of all the wealth in Denmark! As an astronomer, he had new instruments (telescopes and more) built, and was careful about calibrating them to make sure they stayed accurate. He rightfully reasoned that only with these kinds of tools could he study the stars and planets. He was able to observe the orbital patterns of the moon and other heavenly bodies on a regular basis, and as a result, he discovered variations in their paths that others hadn't noticed before. He had a special observatory built near Copenhagen, called Uraniborg, and soon, scientists were praising it as the best observatory in Europe.

But in his personal life, he was definitely, well, unusual. He fought a drunken duel with a student in 1566 and lost part of nose to his opponent's blade. He bought a sculpted fake nose made of gold and silver to wear as a replacement. He always kept a small jar of paste with him to reattach it should it come unglued and fall off. He also employed a dwarf named Jepp as his personal jester. He believed that Jepp had special powers, such as clairvoyance, and had him sit under the table at meal times, and take his own meals there.

But it was his taste in unusual animal companions that caught quite a few people's attentions. He kept a pet moose, or elk. Wait, which one was it? Well, it's all a little confusing. In Swedish the word for moose is *älg*, which, as you can see, resembles "elk." But in North America, a different member of the deer family, the wapiti, is also called an elk. So Americans call the älg a moose, but the British call it an elk, when it is the same species as the moose. But the elk in Europe is not the same as the American elk. All clear? Of course not!

In any case, this majestic animal liked to walk with Brahe, like a dog, and it lived in his castle. Brahe loved showing off the creature to his friends and colleagues, who were no doubt astonished; he was probably very amused. But somewhere along the line, the moose developed a fondness for beer. Seriously. At one point, a nobleman friend of Brahe's asked if he could borrow the animal for a party, where it would no doubt make quite an impression.

Brahe sent the moose over, and everyone was very entertained. And the animal got quite drunk. There isn't a happy ending to this story, sorry to say. The moose got so drunk that it stumbled and fell down a flight of stairs, dying not long after. It was a tragic end for an animal that should never have been kept as a pet to begin with.

GALILEO'S
MISSING BODY PARTS

Galileo (1564–1642) is one of the greatest astronomers in history, famous for his discoveries regarding the planets, the use of the telescope, the proof for a heliocentric model (i.e., that the Earth revolves around the sun), and dropping objects off of the leaning tower of Pisa, which he might or might not have ever done. He also came into conflict with religious authorities over the whole Earth orbit issue, and spent his last years under house arrest. But of course, the truth won out, and now he is revered around the world for his discoveries.

In fact, a lot of people already recognized his greatness in his own time, and after. So much so that at least a few wanted more than just to honor him. In 1737, a full ninety-five years after he died, his body was moved to a new tomb near Michelangelo's in the Santa Croce Basilica in Florence. Up until then, the church had not allowed him to be buried in consecrated ground, because of his so-called controversial teachings. It wouldn't be until 1992 that Pope

John Paul II and the Catholic Church finally apologized to him and admitted their own errors.

When his body was moved, some admirers weren't content to just let him be reinterred, and wanted a piece of the action—literally. Francesco Gori, a collector and lover of all things Roman and Renaissance, decided to retain some souvenirs, so with the help of a few others, they took three of Galileo's fingers, a tooth and a vertebra, using knives, saws, and pliers. They basically treated these pilfered parts as secular versions of holy relics. Maybe they even saw it as fitting, given that Galileo was a kind of "martyr" for the truth.

One of the fingers was donated to Florence, and still resides in the Museo Galileo, effectively giving the finger to everyone that views it. The vertebra ended up at the University of Padua, but the other two fingers and tooth went missing in 1905. They eventually resurfaced in 2009, when the family who owned them decided to put the items up for auction; they had no idea who they belonged to, only that they were very old. And who wants to keep around a pair of old fingers and somebody's tooth, anyway?

A few collectors were interested in the unusual items and did some digging, only to eventually find out who the tooth and digits had originally belonged to, which must have been a shock; by then, historians had concluded that they were lost forever. But they were authenticated, and now all the holy relics of the scientific martyr "St. Galileo" have been found!

ISAAC NEWTON'S
ALCHEMY OBSESSION

Englishman Isaac Newton (1642–1727) ranks as one of the greatest scientists of all time. He made discoveries about gravity (and although the story of the apple falling on his head is untrue, seeing apples fall probably did inspire him to examine gravity), developed the system of differential and integral calculus (students have never forgiven him!), and revolutionized ideas about physics with his laws of motion. He had the good fortune to be born at a time when the Scientific Revolution was getting underway, and there was plenty of support for Newton and his colleagues to carry out experiments and devise new ideas. His 1687 book, *Philosophiae Naturalis Principia Mathematica* (Mathematical Principles of Natural Philosophy) is possibly the most important scientific text in history before the works of Einstein. It sets down his three laws of motion and the theory of gravitation, which explained why planet orbits are elliptical, as well as how the moon orbits the Earth. His use of mathematics in the fields of physics and astronomy was entirely new and groundbreaking.

Newton was a modern man of science, through and through. So it might surprise you to learn that he was also deeply into alchemy, astrology, and even prophecy. Why? Well, in Newton's time, these subjects hadn't yet been banished from academic circles as being "non-serious." Modern chemistry was still in its infancy, so it made sense that a time-honored discipline like medieval alchemy would be worthy of study. In fact, at the time, it was still almost synonymous with chemistry, and was not just about trying to turn base metals into gold or discovering the elixir of life. For Newton, who spent over thirty years of his life studying the subject and wrote something like a million words about it, alchemy was another way to discover answers to the mysteries of the world.

And yet, his writing was done in secret. This was not so much to avoid scorn and derision from his colleagues, but because alchemists were seen as people who had potential value, especially if they'd found ways of changing metals from one form to another. There are stories of alchemists being kidnapped by rulers who wanted to use their secret knowledge, especially if they could create gold or other precious metals. So alchemists tended to keep to themselves and guard their secrets and experiments closely; many were afraid that their ideas and discoveries might be stolen. It seems silly now, but it was a genuine concern back in the day!

As for Newton, he seemed to have a belief that the Earth was constantly generating new metals underground, and that he might be able to replicate the process in his alchemical experiments. But a lot of his notebooks are unclear about what he was doing; he doesn't seem to have been especially interested in trying to turn other metals into gold. However, his use of dangerous chemicals in his alchemy experiments is thought to have brought about another nervous breakdown (he'd already had one previously).

Newton was quite the loner, and apparently a pretty unpleasant man at the best of times. He was regularly getting into arguments and disputes with colleagues, and he had few friends. He also saw himself as smarter than and superior to most other people, which didn't win him any popularity contests. So a secret study of alchemy suited his personality just fine!

BENJAMIN FRANKLIN'S
HOAXES AND PRANKS

Dear old Benjamin Franklin (1706–90) was one of the founders of the United States, a politician, statesman, inventor (of bifocals and the glass harmonica, among other objects), writer, and much more. He was the young nation's ambassador to France for a time, and loved all things French, especially its wine. Everyone knows the story of his flying the kite in the thunderstorm, though in truth, he didn't discover electricity; he used the experiment to prove that lightning was indeed caused by electricity. And some researchers now think the whole story is made up, anyway, like George Washington and the cherry tree.

In any case, Franklin was also fond of literary rivalries, jibes, and attacks. Some people might call him the first troll:

- At the age of just sixteen, Ben wanted to be a writer, but his brother, James, wouldn't publish any of his work in *The New-England Courant*, James' newspaper (that was mean!). So Ben decided to submit a letter under a pen name. He pretended to be a middle aged woman named Silence Dogood. James was impressed and published the letter. This was the first of many such writings about politics and issues of the day. "Silence" even had a few marriage proposals! Needless to say, when James found out, he was not happy!

- Using the fake name "Poor Richard Saunders," Ben created *Poor Richard's Almanack*, and went to work against his main rival, the wonderfully-named Titan Leeds, an astrologer who published *An American Almanack*. As Saunders, Franklin joked that he could predict when Leeds would die, using astrology. It would happen on October 17, 1733, at 3:29 pm, during a conjunction of the Sun and Mercury. Of course, the day came and went and Leeds was alive and well, and he mocked "Saunders." Franklin wrote in response that Leeds had actually died and that someone was writing for Leeds, since the writing was terrible (Leeds had always been a poor writer, by the way). Franklin's trolling drove sales of his publication, and when Leeds eventually did die in 1738, Franklin, as Saunders, simply claimed that the Leeds "imposter" had given up!

- In 1747, Franklin wrote "The Speech of Miss Polly Baker," published in *The General Advertiser* in London. He talked about how Ms. Baker was being put on trial for having a child out of wedlock. The speech asks quite simply: why are the men never held accountable? Intended as a satire, it shone a light on a double standard that was just starting to come into people's awareness, and received a sympathetic response from many readers. Within a few decades, the movement for women's rights would begin, along with increased calls to abolish slavery.

- And on the slavery note, Franklin sent one last letter in 1790 (less than a month before he died) under a false name to *The Federal Gazette*. Calling himself "Historicus," he told of a late seventeenth-century Muslim Algerian ruler named Sidi Mehemet Ibrahim, who advocated for enslaving Christians. His arguments resembled those of pro-slavery congressman, James Jackson, in Georgia, and made Jackson look like a bit of a fool. Did Franklin's prank win anyone over to the cause of abolition? Quite possibly!

ADA LOVELACE
AND THE FIRST COMPUTER

Ada Lovelace (1815–52) was, along with Charles Babbage (1791–1871), a pioneer in early computing. If you've ever opened up a laptop, fired up a desktop, or checked a cell phone, you have these two to thank in part. While they didn't exactly create "Silicon Valley London," Babbage's work in hardware and Lovelace's work with early "software" were major leaps forward in the idea of computing, or rather, inventing a machine that could do complex calculations.

Babbage was an independently wealthy inventor and scientist, while Lovelace was none other than the only legitimate daughter of that original bad boy, Lord Byron. Lady Byron was interested in mathematics and instilled that love in her daughter. She also kept young Ada away from her father so that his "insanity" wouldn't affect her, so there's that. To be fair, he'd already gone off to Greece by then, leaving wife and daughter in Italy.

In 1833, Lovelace met Babbage while he was working on a mechanical calculator he called the Difference Engine. Babbage was so impressed by Lovelace's intellect that he called her the "Enchantress of Numbers." Babbage was also working on another machine, the Analytical Engine, and in 1840, Lovelace was given the task of translating from French to English a speech he'd given in Italy about the machine. She not only translated the talk, but added her own additional commentary in the index, including an algorithm for the machine that some have claimed is the world's first computer program.

But in fact, Babbage had already created similar algorithms back in 1836, meaning that Lovelace wasn't the first. This truth doesn't take anything away from her work, of course, and in fact, she was the one who saw expanded possibilities for what a computer could do. Babbage was mostly concerned with machines that could do math, while Lovelace saw that they could have applications in everyday life. She thought that a machine could be programmed to compose music, for example, and would no doubt be delighted by all of the things computers can do today. She also had a gambling habit and tried to come up with ways that a computer could predict the outcome of horse races, though that didn't work!

Lovelace was an important figure in the days of very early computing and deserves to be honored and remembered for her innovative ideas. While Babbage genuinely respected her, he didn't listen to her on certain topics, and he probably should have, as the computer revolution might have started more than a century earlier!

THOMAS EDISON:
GENIUS, FRAUD, THIEF, OR GOOD BUSINESSMAN?

Thomas Edison (1847–1931) has a reputation as one of the greatest inventors in history, blessing the world with a string of ingenious contraptions that would make our lives better and completely transform the world. He obtained 1,093 US patents in his lifetime, and he left hundreds of other ideas unfinished and unexplored. The so-called "Wizard of Menlo Park" seemed to come up with one thing after another: the alkaline battery, the automatic telegraph, the phonograph, the movie camera, and (of course) the lightbulb. But while he had some definite wins, there was more to the story.

Edison liked to cultivate the idea that he was a lone genius, who labored day and night to come up with innovative ideas that he would then introduce to a public always eager for more. His biggest rival, Nikola Tesla, did something similar. Edison no doubt enjoyed the publicity and attention. But the reality is that Edison didn't come up with ideas in a vacuum; he often built on the ideas and inventions of others, improving them and raising their profile. Of course, some would say that he was actually stealing ideas and taking credit. Did that happen? Quite possibly.

He didn't invent the lightbulb, for example. The concept went all the way back to the 1760s, but the early bulbs never stayed lit for long and were expensive to produce. Edison thought (rightfully) that he could come up with a way to do it, but he had help: a team of assistants who experimented and worked to perfect his ideas. So, not only did he not technically invent the lightbulb, he most definitely didn't do it on his own. But people liked to give him credit, and he was more than happy to take it.

He came up with the idea for the phonograph to record sounds (but not play them back), but he didn't build it himself; he employed a machinist named

John Kruesi to do that part. So again, it was a team effort, but Edison is the one that everyone remembers.

Edison wasn't the only inventor with potentially shady practices. Tesla claimed that he had invented the radio in 1895, and had built a prototype. A fire destroyed his laboratory and a good amount of his work (was the fire deliberately set?). But he was still able to obtain patents for his invention in 1900. At the same time, Italian inventor Guglielmo Marconi filed for a patent on his own version of the radio in 1900, but this was denied since it was too similar to Tesla's. After some back and forth, wherein Tesla claimed that Marconi was using some of his patented ideas, Edison intervened and in 1904, the US Patent Office reversed its decision, and awarded the radio patent to Marconi! Did Edison use his own clout to harm his rival? It seems possible.

Edison did indeed take credit for some things he didn't invent, and sometimes worked on his own versions of existing ideas in secret. So in answer to the question in the entry title—he was actually a bit of all four!

HENRY FORD AND THOMAS EDISON'S
SUPPOSED LAST BREATH

Henry Ford (1863–1947) will forever be remembered for his automobiles (especially the Model T), and the company that still bears his name. Edison will be remembered for his many inventions, though quite a few of them were not his alone, as we've already seen. So what happened when the two of them were together? Something a lot more unusual than you might think.

Ford had worked for the Edison Illuminating Company, eventually becoming a chief engineer, all while tinkering with his car ideas on the side. He presented these ideas to Edison, who, instead of stealing them, was actually impressed, saying something to the effect of "You have it!" The idea of a gas-powered car was apparently something Edison hadn't considered before.

The two became friends and colleagues, even going camping together along with American president Warren Harding. As you do. Over the years that friendship held, and as Edison grew older and weaker, Ford felt some responsibility for him and tried to help where he could.

A strange story has emerged that when Edison was on his deathbed in 1931, Ford went to Edison's son, Charles, and asked him to keep a test tube nearby, so that he could capture Edison's literal last breath in the tube for posterity. Ford had an interest in Spiritualism, and even reviving the dead, and, so the story goes, he might have been trying to capture Edison's soul as it left his body.

This might seem like a bizarre story for two men of science, and it is. The truth is that it probably didn't happen. But since Edison was a chemist and still loved chemistry, his son had eight test tubes placed by his bed as a reminder and a comfort. After Edison's death, Charles later explained, he had one sealed up and gave it to Ford as a token of their friendship.

The tube was lost and then found again in 1950, only to be lost yet again and rediscovered in 1978; it was labelled "Edison's Last Breath?" Why the question mark? Well, it turns out that there are no less than forty-two test tubes at the Edison Estate which are said to hold Edison's last breath; that's quite a lot of breathing as he exited the world! These test tubes begin to resemble medieval holy relics, where there were multiple crowns of thorns, thousands of bits of the true cross, etc.

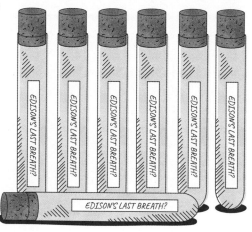

So, do any of them hold Edison's literal last breath? Probably not, but one or more of them might be a tube that was next to him when he died. No word if his soul is trapped inside any of them, though.

MARIE CURIE'S AWARDS AND LONG-LASTING RADIOACTIVITY

Marie Salomea Skłodowska-Curie (1867–1934) was a Polish chemist and physicist, famous for her work with radiation. Along with her husband, Pierre, she discovered polonium, so named because she was from Poland. She and Pierre were awarded a Nobel Prize in Physics for their work in 1903, the first time a woman received the honor, and the first joint award to a couple. Of course, some sexist jerks felt that she should have been excluded, but Pierre, to his credit, insisted that she be honored for all the work she'd done.

Pierre died in 1906 when he was run over by a horse-pulled carriage, but Marie continued with her pioneering work. She discovered an even more radioactive element, radium, and she was eventually awarded another Nobel Prize in 1911, this time in chemistry. She found that radium could kill diseased cells faster than healthy ones, and she proposed that it could be used as an effective treatment for tumors. She was also an advocate for the use of X-rays during World War I, showing that they could be used to better understand a soldier's injury and treat it more effectively.

Winning two Nobel Prizes was an astonishing triumph for a woman in a very male field, where most of those male scientists thought women had no place in research. They probably grudgingly acknowledged her accomplishments, even as they were undoubtedly jealous of her. Incidentally, the Curies' daughter, Irène, would also become a chemist and go on to win a Nobel Prize of her own (with her husband) in 1934. Their other daughter, Ève, became a concert pianist and married a diplomat named Henry Labouisse; he would accept a Nobel Peace Prize on behalf of UNICEF in 1965. Nobels clearly ran in the family!

With all of her accomplishments, it's kind of surprising that Marie didn't seem to fully realize just how danger-ous it was to work with radioactive materials. She was frequently ill, almost certainly due to radiation exposure, and she died in 1934 at the relatively young age of sixty-six, of aplastic anemia, which was caused by radiation. Her experimental laboratory didn't have much in the way of precautions and safety built into it. It never really occurred to anyone that being around so much radiation all the time, even in low levels, was dangerous. She even kept containers of radioactive material on shelves. She wrote: "One of our joys was to go into our workroom at night; we then perceived on all sides the feebly luminous silhouettes of the bottles of capsules containing our products. It was really a lovely sight and one always new to us. The glowing tubes looked like faint, fairy lights."

Very deadly fairy lights!

And it wasn't just her. Several of her papers and a notebook are contaminated with radium, so much so that they are stored in lead-lined boxes at the Bibliothèque nationale in Paris. They're too dangerous to pick up and look through without protective clothing. The boxes even contain some of her cookbooks! Given that radium has a half-life of 1,600 years, they won't be safe for a long time.

NIKOLA TESLA'S
FASCINATING LIFE

Tesla (1856–1943) ranks as one of the more creative and unusual inventors in history. A long-time rival of Thomas Edison, the Serbian-American inventor was known for his work with electricity and inventions such as the alternating current (AC) induction motor, which he licensed to Westinghouse. He was also an early advocate of wireless technology and conducted a number of experiments into its potential uses. Largely forgotten after his death, interest in his work was revived a few decades later. Conspiracy theorists claim that he developed all kinds of mind-bending inventions, including free energy. It seems that some of his patents and notes were confiscated by the American government after his death, so who knows? In any case, here are some fascinating facts about the man behind the legend:

- Appropriately enough, he was born during a lightning storm. Given his obsession with electricity, the world welcomed him in a most fitting way! The midwife thought it was a bad omen, while his mother insisted that the storm was a good sign.

- He had obsessive-compulsive disorder, which was apparent in his dealings with various things. He also hated pearls, saying, "the sight of a pearl would almost give me a fit." He would refuse to talk to women who wore them. He became obsessed with cleanliness and the number three. He was germophobic and would wash his hands three times, while he always had to have eighteen napkins (3x6) on the table when he ate. He was also obsessed with pigeons later in life. There was one in particular, a white bird, which he came to adore. One night, it flew to him through an open window in his hotel room. He said that he saw two points of light in its eyes, and he knew it was dying. Sure enough, it died in his hands. For Tesla, this was a sign that his own life and work were coming to an end.

- He believed he had received radio transmissions from another planet. Tesla was very interested in radio waves and the technology that could develop using them. In 1899 and 1900, he claimed that he was picking up radio messages that could be from Mars, Venus, or perhaps another planet. The *Richmond Times* newspaper (and many others) carried the story in 1901, reporting: "as he sat there one evening, alone, his attention, exquisitely alive at that juncture, was arrested by a faint sound from the receiver – three fairy taps, one after the other, at a fixed interval. What man who has ever lived on this earth would not envy Tesla that moment!" The public was delighted, but scientists scoffed. It's possible that he actually picked up radio transmissions from the experiments of Italian inventor Guglielmo Marconi.

- He worked for Edison, but it didn't go well. Tesla came to America in 1884, and was introduced to Edison, who hired him. He told Tesla that he would give him $50,000 if he could improve on Edison's DC generators. Not long after, Tesla came back and triumphantly told him he'd done so, but Edison refused to pay him. He told Tesla, "When you become a full-fledged American, you will appreciate an American joke." Tesla quit.

ALBERT EINSTEIN:
SO MANY MISATTRIBUTED QUOTES!

Einstein (1879–1955) was arguably the greatest scientific genius that ever lived. His very name is synonymous with absurd levels of intelligence, and his radical new theories overturned much of the physics of Isaac Newton and gave us a wild new concept of how the universe is truly structured (relativity, anyone?). So it stands to reason that he said a lot of smart and profound things. And people love nothing better than posting Einstein quotes in memes, in texts, in videos, or just about anywhere else they can. If Einstein said it, it must be true, right? Everyone wants to have their beliefs backed up by something he said.

Unfortunately, he's one of the biggest victims of misquotes, with a seemingly endless list of fake pearls of wisdom. Here is a list of some of the most common misattributed quotes, things that Einstein never said. The next time you see any of them online, you can roll your eyes and keep scrolling, or you can stop and smugly point out that the original poster has made an error. People love it so much when you do that!

- **"The definition of insanity is doing the same thing over and over and expecting different results."** Possibly his most famous non-quote, it's also been attributed to Ben Franklin and many others. It's one of those quotes that just about everyone likes to use when they are frustrated with the system, but Einstein never said it.

- **"Everyone is a genius. But if you judge a fish by its ability to climb a tree, it will live its whole life believing that it is stupid."** This might be an encouraging bit of advice for those times when we fail or feel useless, but sage advice using animals as teachers dates back to ancient Greece, and Einstein certainly never said this.

- "I refuse to believe that God plays dice with the universe." This one is kind-of-sort-of true. Einstein the agnostic did once say in a letter from 1942: "It seems hard to sneak a look at God's cards. But that He plays dice and uses 'telepathic' methods... is something that I cannot believe for a single moment."

- "Everything is energy and that's all there is to it. Match the frequency of the reality you want and you cannot help but get that reality. It can be no other way. This is not philosophy. This is physics." Would Einstein the physicist really say something like this? Of course not, but it's popular among New Agey and other groups as meme fodder.

- "If the facts don't fit the theory, change the facts." Sigh. See the quote above.

- "Evil is the result of what happens when man does not have God's love present in his heart." This one should immediately set off alarm bells, but it gets bandied around quite a lot. It seems to date from about 1999, and is an example of the "atheist professor" urban legend, wherein the snooty know-it-all non-believing teacher gets bested by his religious student. Definitely not an Einstein quote.

- Finally, here's a quote he really did say. It's lovely and sums up much about the man and his life's work: "The most beautiful experience we can have is the mysterious. It is the fundamental emotion that stands at the cradle of true art and true science. Whoever does not know it and can no longer wonder, no longer marvel, is as good as dead, and his eyes are dimmed."

POLITICS
AND MORE

ELEANOR OF AQUITAINE:
CRUSADER QUEEN AND
MOTHER OF TWO KINGS

Eleanor (1122–1204) is one of the most famous of medieval women. She lived in a time of political turmoil, civil wars, crusades, and rapid change. Women usually had little actual power, and yet she rose above these limitations to become a legend in her own time and afterward. The daughter of Duke William X of Aquitaine, she inherited his lands when he died in 1137, and suddenly became the most eligible bachelorette in Western Europe. She was married first to King Louis VII of France, with whom she went on the Second Crusade in 1147. The marriage was unhappy and the crusade was a disaster for the European forces. After divorcing him in 1152, she married King Henry II of England, with whom she would have five sons, two of which would become kings themselves. She was Queen of France from 1137 to 1152 and Queen of England from 1154 to 1189.

But while her marriage with Henry was a better match, it was no less dramatic. She helped him run his kingdom, which stretched from Scotland in the north to the border with Spain in the south. But Henry was the cheating type, and Eleanor got sick of it. She left England and returned to Poitiers in France in 1167, where she was a noted patron of the arts, establishing her famous "Court of Love." She adored music and poetry, and supported the works of many troubadours, who were poet-musicians based mostly in southern France. Some of them were aristocrats themselves, and they wrote music and poetry of incredible beauty and power that still resonates with modern listeners.

She might have stayed there forever, but in 1173, fed up again with Henry, she backed her son (also named Henry) in a revolt against the king. But Henry II would not be defeated; he put down the rebellion and had Eleanor imprisoned for the next eleven years. She lived a life of luxury, but was not free to travel; it was a kind of royal house arrest. Henry died in 1189, and her son Richard (the Lionheart) freed her and reinstated her to her role as advisor. When he was captured in Germany while returning from the Third Crusade, Eleanor raised the enormous ransom that was demanded for his release (and it was huge!).

Richard died in battle in 1199, and Henry's youngest son, John, then came to the throne. John, as you might know, was not very pop-ular. Eleanor was very old by then, and had less influence on royal matters in England. This meant that John could do whatever he wanted, which was a bit of a disaster that led to the creation of the Magna Carta in 1215 to try to rein him in. Eleanor retired to the abbey at Fontevraud in France, and lived out her final days there, but she was long remembered as a powerful woman whom was not to be crossed.

SYBIL LUDINGTON'S
MIDNIGHT RIDE

"The British are coming!" So shouted Paul Revere as he rode through the night to warn the colonists that the British troops had arrived and all good would-be Americans needed to muster and meet the enemy. Except he never really said that. The colonists considered themselves to be British, and Revere shouting out that the British were coming would have made no sense. Coming from where? Going where? Which British? In any case, Revere did indeed make his famous ride to warn of approaching enemy troops, but he might not have been the only one to stir the young would-be nation.

A young woman named Sybil Ludington (1761–1839) was said to have under-taken a ride of her own. On April 26, 1777, British forces destroyed the town of Danbury in Connecticut, and the next day, colonial and British forces met in Ridgefield. The infamous turncoat Benedict Arnold was present at the battle, though at the time he was still on the American side. Another American commander, Colonel Henry Ludington, was also present, and if the story is to be believed, his sixteen-year-old daughter, Sybil, rode forty miles into the nearby New York area to rally over 400 militia men to come and join the fight.

It's a great story and one that has been repeated by locals as a matter of pride and as a great tourist draw. But did it happen? The problem was that there were no accounts of Sybil's ride from the time. Her story only really began to emerge over 100 years later, in a book from 1880 that cites no sources. This was about the same time as when other women, such as Betsy Ross, were being praised for their roles in the American Revolution. To be fair, this was also the time that Paul Revere himself was starting to become an American icon. So, the tale of Sybil's ride might have been included with the rest—yet another hero in the story of the nation's founding. But again, was it true?

Well, a historian named Vincent Dacquino discovered a letter from Charles Ludington, Sybil's nephew. He wrote in 1854: "My Aunt Sybil [rode] on horseback in the dead of night... to inform Gen'l Putnam."

It's a source from a relative and shows that the tale might have been passed down through the family. The letter doesn't conclusively prove that her ride happened, but the fact that a document some twenty-six years earlier than the 1880 book exists, asking that Sybil be included in a ceremony honoring Revolutionary War heroes is definitely interesting. Charles might have just wanted his aunt to have a bit of fame, but would he really make up something like this? What would be the point? His request suggests that the story was already known, and that he and others believed it to be true.

Sybil's own letters don't mention the ride, but that's not necessarily an issue. She might well have just thought she was doing her duty, and that others were engaged in far greater acts of heroism. The story of Sybil's ride is not proven, but it's certainly possible. As historian Paula Hunt says, "The story of the lone, teenage girl riding for freedom, it seems, is simply too good not to be believed."

THE SUFFRAGETTES:
MARTIAL ARTS MASTERS

As the Victorian age progressed there were many efforts to improve social conditions for the working classes and for women, though they often moved at a very slow pace. One area that continued to be frustrating for women was voting rights. The vote had been expanded at various times in the nineteenth century to allow ever more men to vote, but women were time and again left out, except for some gains like voting in local elections and owning and controlling their own property. By the end of the century, with no big changes, some women had had enough.

An English activist named Emmeline Pankhurst (1858–1928) founded the Women's Social and Political Union (WSPU) in 1903, along with some friends. Their goal was to gain the right to vote for all women, and their motto was "deeds not words." They were going to go out into the world and get into the faces of the authorities to get what they wanted. Of course, these behaviors and general civil disobedience didn't go down so well with those same authorities, and the suffragettes ("suffrage" refers to the right to vote) often found themselves in confrontation with the police. So how did they fight back? By learning jiu-jitsu, of course!

Jiu-jitsu is a Japanese marital art that emphasizes using an opponent's weight and size against them, and was a perfect form of self defense for women having to confront big, angry police officers, especially those officers who got a little too pushy and handsy.

Edith Garrud and her husband William ran a martial arts studio in London, and soon were called on by the WSPU to help teach women some basic self defense. By 1910, Edith was teaching classes in jiu-jitsu specifically to suffragette protestors. It was the perfect solution when these women were being harassed and even attacked by often much larger men. Sylvia Pankhurst, daughter of Emmeline, encouraged all women in the movement to learn the martial art for their own protection. Women began having

jiu-jitsu get-togethers and parties, and you can imagine the surprise of the police and the authorities when these ladies started turning attacks back on them! The press noticed and soon thereafter, some clever writer coined the term "suffrajitsu."

Confrontations only got more heated as the 1910s wore on. Women would heckle politicians and try to disrupt their meetings, which almost always led to police confrontations. And sometimes the responses were violent, with injuries and many arrests, but this often served to sway public opinion in favor of the suffragettes' cause, exactly the opposite of what the grumpy old men in Parliament wanted. Emmeline Pankhurst even had her own squad of women protectors, called the Bodyguard, who fended off police and male attackers with some fancy martial arts moves.

By the time World War I started, most of the suffragettes threw their support behind the war effort, which showed that they were willing to rally for Britain. Many women had to take on jobs formerly done by men (who were off fighting), and so technically, they qualified for the right to vote based on employment. In 1918, the government finally granted the right to vote to women over thirty, and in 1928, the right extended to all women over twenty-one. The suffragettes and their martial arts had triumphed at last!

ELEANOR ROOSEVELT'S
MULTI-FACETED LIFE

Eleanor Roosevelt (1884–1962) was, of course, the wife of President Franklin D. Roosevelt, but she accomplished far more than just being the First Lady, though she did that with grace and talent from 1933 to 1945. She was also a diplomat and activist, and served as the United States Delegate to the United Nations General Assembly after World War II, from 1945 to 1952. Here are some interesting lesser-known facts about this remarkable woman.

- She was a pilot. Roosevelt was inspired by Amelia Earhart and applied for her own pilot's license. The two even flew together once. When Earhart disappeared on her round-the-world flight in 1937, Roosevelt commented, "I am sure Amelia's last words were 'I have no regrets.'"

- She was a syndicated columnist. Between 1935 and 1962, she wrote six articles per week (!), about everything from politics to the war to her personal life. The column was titled "My Day," and she never missed a single week, except after her husband's death in 1945.

- She was committed to helping women in journalism. When she was First Lady, she would hold press conferences for female journalists only, setting a White House precedent and helping to put pressure on newspapers to hire more women. If they wanted access to the First Lady, a paper would need a woman for the job!

- She was an early advocate for civil rights. She attended the Southern Conference for Human Welfare in Birmingham, Alabama in 1938. As usual, seating was segregated, but Roosevelt defied the law and sat next to one of the African American delegates. When told that she needed to move, she moved her chair to be equal in distance between Black and white attendees, and sat back down, defying them. What were they going to do, arrest her?

- She was involved in the drafting of the Universal Declaration of Human Rights. President Truman, who succeeded her husband, appointed her as the American representative to the UN's Human Rights Council in 1946, and she enthusiastically went to work helping to create the document. Truman called her the "First Lady of the World" in recognition of her work and achievements.

- She advertised a variety of items, from hot dogs to margarine. She used the money she made from these services to help with programs for the poor and needy.

- It's thought that her activism was inspired by her secret queer identity. She had at least one female partner (probably more). Her marriage to Franklin became one more of convenience and making a good show for the public, though they still respected and cared for one another. Franklin himself had a number of affairs with other women during their marriage, and this open arrangement seemed to suit them both.

BETTY FORD,
THE TOE-TAPPING FIRST LADY

Betty Ford (1918–2011) is best known as First Lady and wife of President Gerald Ford (from 1974 to early 1977), and later for her work with addiction. Having struggled with alcohol and drug addiction herself, she was open and candid about her battles. She became the first chair of the board of directors of the Betty Ford Center, an organization dedicated to helping others going through the same struggles. She was an advocate for women's issues and a keen supporter of the Equal Rights Amendment. She set the model as one of the first truly politically-active First Ladies, and was genuinely popular with the American people over the years.

What many people don't know about her, though, is that she was a talented and enthusiastic dancer. As a girl in Grand Rapids, Michigan, young Elizabeth "Betty" Bloomer knew that she wanted to dance professionally. She began ballet lessons at the age of eight, and by twelve, she was already teaching children younger than herself how to waltz and do the foxtrot. Her work helped to support her family during the lean years of the Great Depression.

As a teenager, she went to a performance that changed her life. She saw the work of the legendary modern dance choreographer, Martha Graham. She said, "I went to a concert she was doing in Ann Arbor, Michigan; and once I saw Martha in concert with her group in Ann Arbor, my whole idea of dance changed. It had tremendous appeal to me." It changed her views about dance and opened her eyes to what modern dance could really do.

Betty's teacher arranged for her to meet with Graham. The starstruck girl spoke with her and told her that she would love to dance with Graham's company someday. Graham replied that they would love to have her! After high school, Betty moved to Vermont to attend the Bennington School of Dance. She also later studied with Graham in New York. Her dream came true when she had the chance to dance with Graham's company, first as an understudy and then at Carnegie Hall. Parental pressure brought her back to Grand Rapids (they weren't thrilled with the idea of her becoming a professional dancer), and she decided to stay there, rather than going back to New York, but she still wanted to dance and teach, setting up her own group.

She continued to dance throughout her life, and in 1976, as First Lady, she convinced her husband (who happened to be the president, of course!) to award Martha Graham the Medal of Freedom, which honored not only Graham's work, but modern dance as an art form. It was an amazing moment that reunited the two women and gave dance some much-needed and deserved recognition.

ABOUT THE AUTHOR

Tim Rayborn has a keen interest in little-known facts throughout time—the stranger the better! He has written a huge number of books (about forty-five at present!) and magazine articles (more than thirty!), especially on subjects such as music, the arts, general knowledge, all things weird and bizarre, fantasy fiction, science fiction, and history of all kinds. He is planning to write even more books, whether anyone wants him to or not.

He lived in England for several years and studied at the University of Leeds for his PhD, which means he likes to pretend that he knows what he's talking about.

He's also an almost-famous musician who plays many unusual instruments from all over the world that most people have never heard of and usually can't pronounce. He has appeared on more than forty recordings, and his musical tours have taken him across the US, all over Europe, to Canada and Australia, and to such romantic locations as Umbrian medieval towns, Marrakech, Vienna, Renaissance chateaux, medieval churches, and high school gymnasiums.

He currently lives in Washington State with many books, recordings, and instruments. He's also pretty enthusiastic about good wines and cooking excellent food.

www.timrayborn.com

ABOUT CIDER MILL PRESS
BOOK PUBLISHERS

Good ideas ripen with time. From seed to harvest, Cider Mill Press brings fine reading, information, and entertainment together between the covers of its creatively crafted books. Our Cider Mill bears fruit twice a year, publishing a new crop of titles each spring and fall.

"Where Good Books Are Ready for Press"
501 Nelson Place
Nashville, Tennessee 37214

cidermillpress.com